UNDERSTANDING THE ROLE OF EQUITY

Leaders at both the school and district levels need to understand the complexities of equity and its role in order to support their students and staff and to avoid the pitfalls that their colleagues have become victims to due to a lack of knowledge and perspective. Beginning with a foundational understanding surrounding the multifaceted aspects of equity in the school setting, this book supports the researched practitioner with resources and tools to explore policies, practices, and daily decisions that occur as a result. The hands-on approach of case study analysis, followed by the factual review of "what happened" in the actual scenarios, allows for a self-reflective examination of individual decision making and insight concerning what pitfalls to avoid and/or expect. The reflective practice that each leader must strive to perform during their ongoing leadership journey is supported with an introduction to additional theories and subsequent learning concepts.

DAVID T. LINDENMUTH is a faculty member of the College of Education at Rowan University and the Director of the Rowan Institute for Educational Leadership, USA. He has over thirty years of experience working in school districts (ranging from high needs to affluent), preparing students for the opportunities to succeed in various roles, including teacher, counselor, principal, and superintendent. In addition to his background in education, he previously served in the elected positions of city councilman and county commissioner. He was the first county-wide Black elected official in the region.

UNDERSTANDING THE ROLE OF EQUITY

Equity-Focused Case Studies for Education Leaders

DAVID T. LINDENMUTH

Rowan University

CAMBRIDGE
UNIVERSITY PRESS

Shaftesbury Road, Cambridge CB2 8EA, United Kingdom

One Liberty Plaza, 20th Floor, New York, NY 10006, USA

477 Williamstown Road, Port Melbourne, VIC 3207, Australia

314–321, 3rd Floor, Plot 3, Splendor Forum, Jasola District Centre,
New Delhi – 110025, India

103 Penang Road, #05–06/07, Visioncrest Commercial, Singapore 238467

Cambridge University Press is part of Cambridge University Press & Assessment,
a department of the University of Cambridge.

We share the University's mission to contribute to society through the pursuit of
education, learning and research at the highest international levels of excellence.

www.cambridge.org
Information on this title: www.cambridge.org/9781009168007

DOI: 10.1017/9781009168014

First published 2023

A catalogue record for this publication is available from the British Library.

Library of Congress Cataloging-in-Publication Data
NAMES: Lindenmuth, David T., 1969– author.
TITLE: Understanding the role of equity : equity focused case studies for education
leaders / David T. Lindenmuth, Rowan University, New Jersey.
DESCRIPTION: First edition. | New York : Cambridge University Press, 2023. |
Includes bibliographical references and index.
IDENTIFIERS: LCCN 2023019810 (print) | LCCN 2023019811 (ebook) | ISBN
9781009168021 (hardback) | ISBN 9781009168007 (paperback) | ISBN 9781009168014
(ebook)
SUBJECTS: LCSH: Educational equalization – United States – Case studies. |
School administrators – In-service training – United States.
CLASSIFICATION: LCC LC213.2 .L54 2023 (print) | LCC LC213.2 (ebook) |
DDC 379.2/60973–dc23/eng/20230602
LC record available at https://lccn.loc.gov/2023019810
LC ebook record available at https://lccn.loc.gov/2023019811

ISBN 978-1-009-16800-7 Paperback

CONTENTS

It has been a long, and often difficult, complex journey. How did I get to this point? To be writing this book, at this time? Perhaps more importantly, the question should be why.

I have been truly blessed with a wonderful family. One full of love, support, encouragement, and understanding. I want to thank my parents – Verne and Mickey – for all they have done for me. When other children looked to the TV or to the sports field for role models, mine were at home. They provided the daily example that showed me it was admirable to work hard and to treat **everyone** with respect.

> *Train up a child in the way he should go, and when he is old he will not depart from it. Proverbs 22:6*

God could not have given me better parents and I am so thankful to have had them in my life. They allowed this "poor little Black boy" to grow up to teach and lead children, adults, and entire communities.

My mother is the most loving and caring person I have ever known. Her words of encouragement, her special notes, and her spiritual guidance have sustained and nurtured me throughout life's numerous trials and tribulations. My father taught me very early on to value my education. I still remember as an eight-year-old child coming home with a C on my report card in spelling in third grade. He always said he wanted us (my brother and I) to work hard and to do our best.

That day, he knew that a C was not my best. He quickly, and forcefully, told me that if "my skinny little *$# (you fill in the blank) ever wanted to play football again (playing football was my life at the time and would be so up into my 20s), that I better never bring home a report card like that again." From that day on, I was an honor student. Thanks! I only wish you were still here to see my continued path along this journey.

To my wife and children, Wow!!!! I thank God for each of you every day. Thank you for the patience, understanding, and encouragement. Thank you for giving me time when I need peace and quiet and for not letting me sit in silence when I need to talk. I don't know what I would do without you and I never want to find out. You are the source of my inspiration and give me great pride in all that you are, in all that you have done, and in all that you will do.

The aforementioned journey has taken me to some surprising and unexpected stops, with many firsts along the way. I have spent thirty-plus years working in a wide range of P-12 public school districts (from affluent to "high needs") in various positions. I've been a teacher (Math in both the MS and HS settings), a school counselor, a coach (football at the HS and collegiate levels, as well as basketball and track and field at the HS level), an assistant principal, a principal, and a superintendent. In addition to my education background, in what seems like a different lifetime, I previously held elected office as a city councilman and county "commissioner" allowing insight into the behind-the-scenes politics that affect the education world. A common thread intertwined throughout these experiences is how important it is to have an understanding regarding the role of equity at all levels of society. Or sadly, how damaging a lack of understanding or concern regarding equity can be for all involved.

The examples and lessons learned throughout my career are numerous, but allow me to review a select few.

Early on in my teaching career, I was one of only two non-White teachers (the only academic teacher) in the entire middle school where I was teaching. The overwhelming majority (90 percent) of my students were White. Like most new teachers, I did some things well and some things maybe "not so well." Overall, I looked at this particular year as a success and enjoyed my students. On the last day of school, one of my students, "Sally," walked up to me just before the bell rang and handed me a note and told me to have a nice summer. With the chaos that is the last day of school, I did not get a chance to read Sally's note until the school day had ended and everyone had left for the summer.

Sally was a good student. She had just moved into the district and this was her first year in a new school. She was quiet, but seemed to quickly make friends and become acclimated in her new school environment. I'm sure that she was nervous when she started in our school. Her note would enlighten me as to why she was nervous.

Sally began her note by thanking me for a wonderful school year. She stated that she learned a lot and really enjoyed it. My class was her favorite! She said she was so nervous to start the year, especially when she found out that I was going to be one of her teachers. In her words, the reason she was so nervous was because she had never had a **Black teacher** before. She was so afraid that I would be mean and treat her poorly. She wanted to thank me for being nice, caring, and a good teacher.

The new shy, quiet, little girl was more nervous about having a Black teacher than she was about starting in a brand new school with no friends. The young naïve teacher that I was at the time was quickly reminded that I am often looked at differently before I even open my mouth and that I need to be prepared for these judgments.

As I stated earlier, football played a huge role in my life. While playing football, I had several coaches who were excellent role models and instrumental in my life. Unfortunately, I have also had the opposite as well. One day, one of my college coaches was talking with some of the other players about his new car. One of my teammates was telling the coach how nice the car looked and how much he liked it. During the conversation, the coach looked at me and asked me if I saw his new car. I told him I did not.

As a side note, I really didn't care for this coach because I didn't really think he cared for me. I couldn't quite put my finger on it, but there was something that didn't quite feel right. What he said next would make everything just a little bit more clear.

> He said, "You gotta go check my car out after practice, Lindenmuth. . . . I bet you'll love it!"
> I said, "OK, Coach."
> He responded, "I mean it, I know you'll love it, Lindenmuth. It's a BMW!"
> I again said, "OK, Coach."

He then said, "You know what BMW stands for, don't you, Lindenmuth?"

Annoyed, I said, "No, what does it stand for, Coach?"

He laughed and said, "It stands for **Black Man's Wish**! So make sure you go check it out because you're never gonna have one! (while laughing)."

At that moment the head coach signaled for everyone to move to the next part of practice.

As a football player your coach is someone you look up to as almost a second father. It is someone you look to for guidance and want to make proud. Here I was smacked in the face with the fact that this man I was supposed to run through a brick wall for didn't really think too much of me as a person. Even at this place where we were all supposed to be on the same team and a family, I learned that some people in places of authority will never view me as worthy.

When I was a school superintendent, I was often the only Black superintendent in the county and/or region. No matter the district, I always believed that it was part of my responsibility as a leader to be involved at the regional and state level to help move things forward for all students and the profession as well. True leaders want to be part of the solution and work to make things better, not just sit around and complain.

After one particular meeting of a state committee, I voiced my concern to the leader (we'll call him Rick) of the state organization regarding the need to offer more support for Black and Latinx leaders. "Rick's" response was, "What would we really do? There's only a couple of you?" And then he promptly walked away to go to lunch.

To some in authority, there is no urgency to change things or attempt to address "your" issues concerning equity because they don't really affect them, until it does affect them. And then, it's too late.

I had the great honor of being elected the first Black person (or any non-White person) to hold the position of county commissioner where I resided. I held the position for two terms (until the superintendency became too much of a demand – as a side note, I never lost an election ☺) and was selected to be Deputy Director for three of my six years in office.

One evening, after a meeting, some of my colleagues decided to go out for a drink. These were men I had worked with for multiple years and had good relationships with. One of them (Jim) asked me to join them for a quick drink at the local "Elks Lodge" to celebrate the outcome of the evening's meeting as we came out ahead on a particularly contentious topic. Before I could even offer my answer of no, our other two colleagues quickly pulled Jim to the side to firmly, but quietly, tell him something. Jim was visibly flustered and stated that he "was not going then" and walked with me in the other direction toward my car.

During the walk to the car, Jim apologized to me repeatedly and told me he didn't know. I asked him what he was talking about. He told me he didn't realize that the lodge didn't serve "Blacks." He was appalled and shocked that the others who would go there on a regular basis, knew this.

No matter the title or position, to some I will always be "just" a Black man in a suit. Even those that may, on the surface, appear to be supporting me or smiling and patting me on the back would rather live in a separate and unequal society.

I offer these examples only to give you an insight into "my" why. Anytime we want to pretend that equity or the lack thereof is not an issue, we will quickly and painfully be reminded that it is a present and constant struggle. As leaders, we can't ignore injustices and only act when they smack us in the face or make our jobs more difficult. It is our responsibility to act, to grow, and to try to understand. This is why we are here.

Why Equity?

Why?

Why Education Leaders? Why Equity? Why Case Studies? Why this book?

There is no better place to start any exploration than by asking the question WHY? Without knowing, and truly understanding, the why, any solution or path selected will not reach its true potential or become truly "successful." Unfortunately, when actions and/or initiatives are put in place, the why is rarely, if ever, considered, contemplated, or discussed. It should not be a surprise then that when these same initiatives are replaced on the merry-go-round of "the next big thing," that they are met with an accompanying response of "here we go again" from the staff members who are tasked with doing the work behind the leader's "new idea." This work is too important not to begin with a strong foundation. It is too important not to begin with the WHY. As a way to ground the thought processes of leaders on the "why" – regardless of the issue or concept – Simon Sinek's *Golden Circle* offers a visual model to redirect leaders (see Figure 1.1) (Sinek, 2011).

All too often leaders begin with the "What" and the "How." "What speaker should we bring in to 'talk' about *Equity*?" ... "What program is the best way to teach about *Diversity*?" ... "What is the best model for *Inclusive*

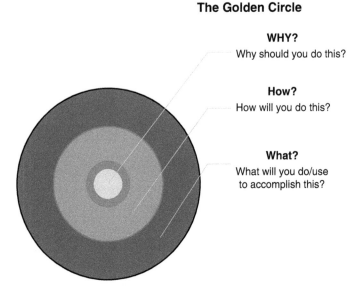

Figure 1.1 The Golden Circle

Practices?" ... "How are we going to implement and incorporate this into our school or district?" ... And the one that stops many a well-meaning discussion in its tracks, "How are we going to pay for this?"

While these questions can all be valid (more or less), unless there is a solid answer to the "Why" question, when difficult conversations and tough times come – and they will come – the path forward will likely be blocked and abandoned to focus on some other "important" task. To begin with the "why" regarding this book's purpose and discussion, one must begin with examining the "why" regarding the core purpose and goal of education as a whole.

Various scholars, educators, politicians, and statesmen with far greater notoriety and influence than I have discussed and debated the goal of education. The likes of Thomas Jefferson and Benjamin Franklin looked to education to be the breeding ground for the future strength of a democratic society. The nation's citizens must understand how a democracy works and hold dear to its concepts and their role in it. This would allow the nation to grow and prosper, providing for a better life and future for all.

W. E. B. Dubois and Booker T. Washington saw education as a chance to strive for equity and an opportunity. An opportunity to overcome the hatred and oppressions endured for generations. Through education, the oppressed could build a better life and future for themselves and their families. An education could unlock the door to endless possibilities and hope. Additionally, a well-educated majority would not allow for the evils of past generations to continue.

John Dewey's progressive education model was both pragmatic and democratic. It focused on the needs of the student. Doing so would assist in the future success of the child. Educators needed to understand and appreciate what students were experiencing and what they would need to be successful. A student's perspective and desires are paramount in attaining true success.

Scholars of today like Yong Zhao state that the American education system should be a place to develop an innovative and entrepreneurial mindset in students so that they can not only compete but also be leaders in a global society. Accordingly, the world of education must embrace the creativity and ingenuity of the American education

3

system. Taking all of this into account, the espoused goal presented here is that the overarching purpose of education is *to prepare students for the opportunities of the future.*

Opportunities are the gateway to success. Often, exposing students to opportunities can be a teacher's greatest success. Whether it is a student in a high school or when dealing with adults preparing to become teachers or administrators, it is found that unless they know what the possibilities are they can never completely strive for true excellence.

The key is to insure that all students are being prepared to take advantage of those opportunities when they present themselves. In life, and especially in the world of education, one rarely gets any advance notice of when the next "great thing" is about to happen. Students must be given the tools and the accessibility to be able to take advantage of those opportunities – a new way of accomplishing a task, a new skill set, a new job, a teachable moment, and so on.

In today's educational environment, learning needs to be real and purposeful. As Zhao states, schools must intentionally design learning experiences which are meaningful, challenging, and purposeful for students (Zhao, 2009). It is about creating something new based on an exploration of possibilities that requires a "discipline of planned abandonment" or letting go of the old in order to create something new (Senge, 2000).

The need for collaboration in all aspects of society is evident. "Teamwork" plays a vital role in all work environments. It is not uncommon at work to be on a team with members in different cities, states, and/or even countries. Students need to not only be comfortable working in teams, but also master the skill of doing so. It has been stated that the objective of the education system in the United States is to prepare students for success in their chosen vocation/profession and to be productive members in a democratic society (Dewey, 1921; Government Printing Office, 1918; Aikin, 1942; Zhao, 2009).

Learning from and with each other is key – there are many different perspectives to all issues and understanding them leads to a deeper understanding, and in turn learning, and often results in the discovery of several different "correct" answers. The diversity of the American education system should be a source of pride and should be viewed as an important resource. It is a skill that needs to be cultivated and nurtured. Workplace diversity is more valued than ever and as such has proven to be more productive (and profitable) than ever (Shemla, 2022).

Students need to be able to pull the best and most useful information from all involved. The phrase "no man is an island" has never been more true than it is in today's society. Working with various stakeholders is a skill: one that needs to be cultivated throughout the education process, not one that individuals try to master once they enter the world of work.

The Eight-Year Study taught that the end goal in education should not be to teach all students the same thing, but to give them meaningful and purposeful exposure for life (Aikin, 1942). Additionally, Tanner and Tanner (2007) state that curricula should be focused on issues that students face and consider important. A global society will require that students collaborate with others on a daily basis. Students communicate on Twitter, Instagram, and so on with people from all around the world. They collaborate with people they've never met before to team up to play and "beat" a game on their PlayStation or Xbox. If they need to find the answer to a dilemma, they can easily collaborate with hundreds, if not thousands, of "friends" online to find a solution. "Friends" of varying backgrounds, races, ethnicities, and so on, just "friends."

"Alone we can do so little; together we can do so much." – Helen Keller

As the Eight-Year Study taught us, schools must meet the needs of the student and the larger society in a democratic manner (Aikin, 1942). So much of what takes place in society is based on the message and how it has been communicated. Students need to be effective communicators in order to compete and succeed. Zhao speaks of helping to create a generation of entrepreneurs (2009). Students need to be able to get their message out; they need to be able to express their thoughts and points of view and to do so with all different kinds of people.

The history of education does give some insight to what has been proven to work though. The Eight-Year Study (sometimes referred to as the Thirty-School Study) was conducted by the Progressive Education Association from 1930 through 1942 (I know that is not an eight-year span, but focus). Thirty high schools redesigned their curricula to include innovative practices in testing, program assessment, student guidance, course sequencing, and staff development.

The Eight-Year Study began under some of the same external pressures that are seen in today's environment, but it

WHY?

demonstrated that giving students freedom and autonomy produced greater success than a **tightly focused curriculum or *standards***. In fact, students from the most experimental schools earned greater academic achievement rates than students from traditional schools. It also showed that when the backgrounds, experiences, and needs of the students were taken into consideration, all flourished.

Similarly, the Cardinal Principles of Secondary Education (1918) concluded that "education should be determined by the needs of the society to be served, the character of the individuals to be educated, and the knowledge of educational theory and practice available." The Cardinal Principles were the work of the Commission on the Reorganization of Secondary Education. The focus of the commission was to analyze secondary education in America.

The commission's findings were key in starting a standard of forming goals before reforming schools. Schools should take into account the individual backgrounds, differences, goals, attitudes, and abilities of their students (sound like student-centered?). The concept of democracy was decided on as the guide for education in America.

These two studies give us guidance as to where our education system should be moving toward. One can go as far as to refer to them as The Declaration of Independence (Cardinal Principles) and The Road Map to Achieve Success (Eight-Year Study) of the American education system – grounded in embracing the uniqueness of our students and in supporting all of them.

In the words of the Rev. Dr. Martin Luther King, "an individual has not started living until he can rise above the

7

narrow confines of his individualistic concerns to the broader concerns of all humanity." Educators must embrace the diversity, creativity, and innovative spirit of the students of today. Educators, and society as a whole, should embrace and strive to enhance every child's strength, not just try to fix their problems or deficits. As John Dewey stated, education programs that do not let students learn, grow, and create **together** "defray the democratic dream and reduces the possibilities of progress."

Education leaders must first want to understand the backgrounds and experiences of those they work to support and guide. (An important note of emphasis – "wanting to understand" is key. One can know all the theories and statistics, but if one doesn't **want to understand,** then there will be little progress and real change.) Leaders must truly value the varied perspectives that their students and staff bring to the learning table as all can grow and benefit from the lived experiences of the group.

Many well-meaning individuals will remind colleagues to teach, and live, according to the "Golden Rule" – *treat others the way you want to be treated.* Some will mistakenly even translate that approach into their schools and classrooms *to teach others the way you want to be taught.* But that concept makes an assumption that is made all too often in our society. It assumes that the way "you," or the way the majority, want things to be done or spoken or presented is the "correct" way to do things. It discredits and de-values the thoughts, preferences, and needs of "others." Instead, an alternative "rule" is offered to be followed that is much more inclusive and embraces that students and staff come from various backgrounds, cultures, and experiences. Instead of the "Golden Rule," what if leaders followed the "Platinum Rule" – treat others the way THEY wish to be treated? Treat, teach, and lead in the manner that individuals (the others) desire. Include and value where they are and where they come from and where they want to attain to – want to understand, appreciate, and value them and their struggles.

How?

Now that the "Why" has been explored (and that a personal and reflective process of exploration regarding one's individual why has begun), it is appropriate to examine the "How."

Leadership isn't easy. Leadership, in the true sense of its meaning, isn't easy. Leadership is much more than the name or title on the door or the signature line of an email. It is constant. Leadership is an ongoing journey, not a destination. To be good at it, one must always be working at it – looking for ways to improve, always striving to learn more. It isn't for the faint at heart, and if the goal is to be "liked by all," then leadership is definitely the wrong "vocation."

Current and future leaders must constantly reflect upon their practices and strive to hone their skills in an effort to serve all students and stakeholders in an equitable manner. Maintaining high expectations, while creating and sustaining equitable and supportive learning environments, is part of the duties of the true educational leaders of today. Successful leaders continue to push and explore topics in an effort to gain insight and understanding. Case studies are an excellent tool to assist with that exploration.

Case studies give leaders the exposure to real-life messiness that they may not encounter – or better said, have not encountered as of yet – in their current environment. The idea behind case study analysis is to use real-life examples and scenarios to "practice" the application of theory while developing an understanding of the true causes to the "issues" that abound throughout education. Additionally, as part of this text's purpose, case studies allow leaders to dig a little deeper into the underlying causes to examine the role of equity that often gets overlooked in the frantic "next on the list" day of a typical school administrator.

After Chapter 2 of this text, you will be given a series of case studies. Each case study will present a scenario based on a real-life situation encountered in a P-12 school district/school in the United States. Names and locations will be changed, but the events and details will be factual. As part of the structure of this book, the reader will be asked how they would respond if they were the administrator in charge. "Guiding questions" will be given to assist the reader as they navigate the environments and those involved. Finally, each case study will end with a "So, What Happened?" section that will detail how the real-life event played out and what was the end result as it relates to the course of action taken by those in charge. In some instances, some connections to theories and additional learning opportunities will be explored and presented.

These case studies can be utilized in several formats. If working individually or in a class setting, the expectation is that one will analyze each case study and then "write up" the said analysis, including a recommended course of action.

A suggested method or protocol for analyzing case studies will be presented shortly. The key will be to explore the role of equity in each scenario, even when it is not so "obvious" at the onset.

The case studies can also be utilized in a Professional Learning Community (PLC) setup or a Professional Development offering. Participants could be "assigned" to complete different aspects of the case study protocol (forthcoming) and/or to view the case study from various perspectives or the viewpoints of different stakeholders. The key is the discussion that results and the examination of the role of equity in each. Sometimes it may be several layers below the surface, but it is important to keep digging.

Now, the "What"

Once one has read and taken in (and discussed) the information from the case study, what comes next? What does one do with it? The analysis of the case study and the reflection and exploration that results is an excellent opportunity for personal growth and the expansion of a leader's competencies. This analysis must be pointed and purposeful. The mere reading of a case study and peripheral pondering of the events is not nearly enough.

Many have offered various methods for this analysis, some quite good and useful. For instance, Gorski and Pothini (2018) offer a very good seven-step process for analyzing educational case studies. For the most part, there is no right or wrong way to analyze a case study just as long as one is satisfying the task or purpose of the exercise as it is laid out.

As part of this text, the following Case Study Analysis Protocol (see Figure 1.2) is offered. One of the rationales for this protocol is that the "steps" or processes can be useful and

READ

Critically read through the entire Case Study and then go back and re-read it. Make notes and/or highlight important facts or issues to be addressed. Define the problems that need to be addressed.

REMOVE

Once the READ phase is complete, REMOVE yourself from the situation. Take a break from the Case Study – and then contemplate…

RESTATE

With a clear mind, go back and RESTATE or summarize the Case Study as if explaining it to a trusted colleague or peer. Focus on and share the pertinent facts. Explain and elaborate on what the "problems" (or "possibilities") are.
Who are the victims? Are there any "unintentional" victims?

REMEDIES

Begin to make a list of possible remedies or courses of action. Do not stop with the first or best "solution". Even if, at first blush the solution appears to be "not a great choice" include it on your list. Truly brainstorm.

How would each be implemented? Who would be involved?
Describe the steps that would be taken

RESPOND

Respond to the Case Study by selecting the best possible solution. It is vital to not only explain the solution but to also explain the "why" behind that solution. Elaborate on who the solution helps and how it addresses the various issues (both at the surface and below).

Identify and discuss any possible issues or pitfalls.

Figure 1.2 The 5R Case Study Analysis Protocol

applied in the "live" and ever fluid world of school leadership. Each step of the protocol builds upon the prior steps to give a cumulative "end product" that informs recommended plans of action. As a result, informed, reflective, and equitable practices and solutions can be offered to the multifaceted situations that schools and leaders face daily. In the end, it's not enough to just run around and "put out the daily fires" of a school day. Many school leaders spend countless hours "managing" or trying to "contain" the same repeat behaviors or problems every day. True educational leaders must look to find solutions to problems before they become "problems."

Case Study Analysis Protocol

READ – It sounds simple enough. Begin by reading each case study. But it goes a little deeper than just that. Critically read each case study. Read through the entire case study completely and then go back and reread it. On the second time through begin to take notes and/or highlight important facts or issues to be addressed.

Define the problems that need to be addressed. (There is always more than one problem to be addressed.) Why do they exist? What is the history behind them? Who do they affect? Begin to make a list of the stakeholders involved/affected in the scenario. Be sure to expand your traditional "vision" here. There is never really a narrow band of damage regarding "problems" in schools. It's never as simple as it looks. There is a wide range of both issues and of those involved/affected concerning school "problems."

Outside of a case study analysis, this step might be renamed LISTEN. In an active school environment, the first step for the

---

leaders involved will be to listen. To be effective though, the leader must actively listen and take in all information and want to accept all perspectives of those involved. Again, it's never as simple as one may originally think or as easy as one may want it to be. By actively listening, and resisting the temptation to quickly "fix" the "daily fires" that present themselves, leaders can begin to truly understand the issues being presented and work to develop sustainable equitable solutions. These solutions can prevent present problems from reoccurring while at the same time prevent future problems from ever becoming problems.

REMOVE – Once the READ phase is complete, REMOVE yourself from the situation. Take a break from the case study – take a walk around the building, work on another issue/task, visit a classroom. Remove your focus from the case study. It doesn't have to be a long break, but nevertheless, take a break.

Oftentimes, leaders can get caught up in the daily grind and in "crossing things off the list" as they go through the day. This just adds to the mindset of constantly putting out the daily fires. Leaders need to give their minds time to "explore" and even "play" with a scenario internally to completely see the problem and possibilities that have been presented. In another setting, this author references the concept of leaders having a "**genius space**" to work through issues and options in this manner.

Problem or Possibility? It is easy to get caught up in the "daily fire" mindset. Leaders think, "I have so many things on my list," and attempt to fix every problem as quickly as possible.

Leaders must take the time to slow down and to try to view the various situations as Possibilities rather than as Problems. If they are narrowly viewed as only problems to be quickly fixed or taken care of, they will undoubtedly return in the near future and over and over again (daily fires). If leaders can in turn examine the Possibilities that can be explored while investigating the same situations, equitable practices and solutions can be put in place to eliminate repeat situations of a similar nature.

Leaders must take the time to allow their minds to contemplate the possibilities that every situation offers. Spending a little more time here can save valuable time going forward by avoiding repeat situations or issues. More importantly, it can help minimize preventable suffering and/or inequity for students, staff, and the entire school community.

RESTATE – With a clear mind, go back and RESTATE or summarize the case study as if one was explaining it to a trusted colleague or peer. Focus on and share the pertinent facts. Explain and elaborate on what the "problems" (or "possibilities") are.

Make it a point here to internally ask the question: Are there any "unintentional" victims? Typically, the intended victim or victims in a scenario are obvious. But, as stated previously, it's never as simple or as quick as it may first seem. Again, dig deeper. As the saying goes, "Is it better to go a mile wide and an inch deep or a mile deep and an inch wide?" In most cases, it's best as a leader to go "a mile deep." Real growth and sustainable solutions are found after excavating several layers of "stuff" in the school environment. During this RESTATE step, one may need to take out the shovel and dig deeper.

REMEDIES – Begin to make a list of possible remedies or courses of action. Indeed, it should be a list. Do not just stop with the first "solution" thought of or with the one that appears to be the obvious "best way" to proceed. Even if at first blush the solution appears to be "not a great choice," include it on your list. Think of all possible remedies and list them. Truly brainstorm.

With each possible solution, begin to add details as to what each would entail. How would each be implemented? Who would be involved? Describe the steps that would be taken and the time frame. An important next step is to explore (and note) who does each "remedy" help and who does it hurt. Identify a list of pros and cons. Again, to answer these questions thoroughly, the leader will need to go below the surface and really examine all of the moving parts of each possible solution.

RESPOND – Once the prior steps are completed, it is time to respond to the case study by selecting the best possible solution. It is vital to not only explain the solution but leaders will also need to clearly explain the "why" behind that solution. Elaborate on who the solution helps and how it addresses the various issues (both at the surface and below) that the scenario presents.

Finally, it is extremely important to identify and discuss any possible issues or pitfalls associated with the determined course of action. No matter how "great" the solution or remedy, there are usually issues that could result due to the actions to take place. What are the unintended consequences? Leaders need to be prepared for the "unexpected." Oftentimes, leaders are remembered on how they handled the "unimaginable." For school leaders, there needs to be Plan A, Plan B, Plan C, and so on for all situations.

It is important to acknowledge that in the midst of the chaos, leaders often do not have the time to go through each of the steps as presented and discussed. The purpose is not to memorize and follow the steps verbatim. The hope is that with enough practice, the reflective and equity practices utilized in reviewing case studies will become second nature. As the saying goes, practice makes perfect. Although the case studies supplied in this text may not offer any absolute correct or "right" answers, they are designed to assist leaders in understanding how to ask the right questions and in remembering what perspectives and options need to be considered.

2

An Understanding

A common point of discussion (and even heated debate) in educational leadership circles is the debate concerning if it "better" to be a researcher or a practioner. Is it more valuable to know, study, and be involved in research, or is the day-to-day interaction of being in the field as a practioner of more value? The answer is quite an obvious one – YES.

To be the effective and transformative leader that students and schools need, leaders must be both. At both the district and building level, practicing administrators are practioners, but they need to be well versed in literature, current research, and how they may be applied in their positions to allow students and teachers to flourish. They need to be *researched practioners*.

A researched practioner is more than just the principal who reads the occasional magazine article or listens to the "hot new" podcast. The researched practioner is one who makes reading and learning an integral part of their routine. Not only are the established and core fundamentals part of their knowledge base, but new and emerging research is also constantly explored and analyzed to enable its inclusion in the leader's toolbox.

The researched practioner does not stop there though. They take the vital step of analyzing their current environment and practices along with reflective practice as action research methods. The same way an NFL coach may "self-scout" their own team to look for tendencies and efficiencies – and perhaps more importantly, inefficiencies. The researched practioner is constantly evaluating and reexamining their individual actions/practices along with those of their school/district. The researched practioner is forever "monitoring and adjusting" the strategies, programs, and procedures of themselves and of those around them.

With the goal of being researched practioners in mind, this chapter will focus on gaining an underlying and foundational understanding of the concepts that will be relied upon during the examination of the role that equity plays in the forthcoming case studies. It is important to note that this is an attempt to share fundamental information and background. By no means will you become "researched" based on this one chapter or even the entire book. At its core, being a researched practioner is a constant mission. It is vital to understand that leadership itself is ever evolving. Leadership is an ongoing journey and not a destination.

Another important realization is that it's OK not to know everything. As a researched practioner, leaders need to accept the fact that they do not, nor will they ever, know everything. That is part of the "researched" component of being a researched practioner. They will be constantly learning (life-long learner) and embracing a growth mindset – always learning and growing. As they do this, a very important "by-product" is the example that they provide for their staff. By modeling this growth mindset and self-awareness and the need for more understanding, the researched practioner is demonstrating the practices that their teachers and fellow administrators should be taking in order to grow and to become truly successful.

Building an Understanding

The benefits of diversity are numerous and abound throughout research. The United States is founded upon the principles of inclusion and embracing the differences that make its citizenship truly "American." Having diversity in the makeup of student populations in schools has proven to increase creativity, empathy, caring, future success, and the overall well-being of students (Zhao, 2009).

According to the writings of Thomas Jefferson (who, granted, had his own issues surrounding the concepts of equity and diversity) and John Dewey, the father of the American education system, the purpose of education is the sharing of social experiences so that children become integrated into the democratic community, ensuring a community that embraces and appreciates its differences in all forms.

To begin any discussion or exploration, it is imperative to have some foundational background knowledge and understanding of the present-day situation in schools.

The Achievement Gap

The "Achievement Gap" refers to the performance disparity between different groups of students. It presents its self along racial, gender, and socioeconomic boundaries. It is manifested when analyzing standardized test scores, dropout rates, course selection trends, and other measures of accomplishment (Ansell, 2011). The Achievement Gap is real and it is not just a phenomenon in the United States. It has been studied and confirmed in numerous other countries, including Canada and the United Kingdom (Ferguson, Bovaird, and Mueller, 2007).

It would be neglectful not to acknowledge the problem and inherent issue with just the term "Achievement Gap." Most immediately think of "those poor students" who are "at risk" and/or lost and "left behind." "How can we fix them?" Sadly, deficit thinking and language abound throughout education. Deficit thinking is rooted in a blame-the-victim mentality that suggests that students/people are responsible for their predicament and fails to acknowledge that they live within coercive systems that cause harm with no accountability (Davis and Museus, 2019). In his critically acclaimed masterpiece *The Souls of Black Folks*, W. E. B. Du Bois (1903) ponders the "Negro problem" and how it feels to be a "problem." He eloquently explains that it is not he and his race that are the "problems" that need to be solved or "broken people" who need to be fixed. It is in fact the institutional structures, policies, and procedures that have marginalized and alienated entire communities and groups and prevented them from having access to opportunities for success. As we consider the Achievement Gap (and other concepts), it is crucial that we examine it with an anti-deficit perspective that would suggest that racially minoritized students are not "at risk," but educational institutions are at risk of failing them.

Research regarding the Achievement Gap is not a new concept. A study of low-income minority and middle-income White students explored the gaps in academic achievement (Berliner, 2006, 2009), and the "Equality of

Educational Opportunity Report," or the "Coleman Report," as it was more widely known, suggested that both school and home/community factors contribute to the Achievement Gap. The research further details how different factors affect children from low-income backgrounds significantly as compared to those from middle-income families.

Data shows that these "gaps" exist on multiple levels. When one examines race, gender, income, and language, clear gaps of various increments emerge. For better or worse, the research clearly indicates that the most significant gaps in achievement are associated with race and income. But what do the numbers specifically show?

In New Jersey, an examination of the 2015 Partnership for Assessment of Readiness for College and Careers (PARCC) results show that the state's graduation requirement assessment reveals glaring deficiencies attributed to the "Achievement Gap" (McKillip and Luhm, 2020). The "passing rates" for the HS English Language Arts 11, a graduation requirement, indicate that only 52 percent of Black and 57 percent of Hispanic students passed, while 69 percent of White students passed. Similarly, the passing rate of economically disadvantaged students was 55 percent. That was 15 percent lower than that for noneconomically disadvantaged. Statewide, the passing rate for high-income districts was 78 percent; for middle-income districts it was 64 percent; and for low-income districts it was only 50 percent.

Research and data confirm that the Achievement Gap is real, but the question remains, what is the cause? Incredibly, in the 1990s, there was a theory that the Achievement Gap was a result of genetic makeup: an assertion that has been widely discredited and scorned (Johnson and Viadero, 2000). Other researchers have since acknowledged that such thought is not credible. Additionally, researchers have recognized that racism has become more subtle and is becoming more difficult to recognize and combat such that racism may now "exert its negative influence with relative ease and impunity" (Chin, 2010). But the fact that it was ever a "theory" is troubling and concerning in its own right.

Another study showed that there is no difference in inherent cognitive ability between different races; but rather, the root cause of the Achievement Gap is more likely socioeconomic in nature (Dickens, 2005). Most experts concur and believe that the Achievement Gap is caused by a combination of poverty, poor health, limited resources, the lack of opportunities, access, exposure, and other environmental factors when comparing the poor and the wealthy. These households, and hence the experiences of the children in them, are completely different. Studies have shown that children raised in poverty whose parents can provide engaging learning environments at home do not have the same Achievement Gap discrepancies as evident among poor children in general (Sparks, 2011).

When examining this complex issue that has plagued educators, and in searching for successful strategies to reduce, and ultimately eliminate, the effects of the Achievement Gap, one must break it down into its various underlying components. Different experts will approach the Achievement Gap in different ways. The approach taken here in exploring the Achievement Gap is to understand that it is actually made up of three underarching gaps: the Opportunity Gap, the Confidence Gap, and the Honesty Gap (Figure 2.1).

The Underlying Gaps

(that make up the *"Achievement Gap"*)

Opportunity Gap

The manner in which race, ethnicity, socioeconomic status, English proficiency, community wealth, familial situations, or other factors can contribute to lower educational aspirations, achievement, and attainment for students (Abbott, 2014).

Confidence Gap

"Your ability and your aptitude, will not affect your altitude, as much as your attitude."

A lack of confidence can also come from within. students can experience a lack of confidence as a result, fearing that they will be judged to have traits that are associated with negative stereotypes of their race, gender, or ethnic group. This fear can cause a type of "toxic stress" (Steele, 1998).

Honesty Gap

The biases that cause individuals (often unaware and unintentionally) to view some as less capable than others. The honesty gap has to do with a lack of self-reflection by individuals regarding how their biases and preconceived perceptions of others can limit the success and achievement levels of the groups affected. The honesty gap can steal future opportunities, causing some to "live up" to the low expectations set before them.

Figure 2.1 The underlying gaps

The Opportunity Gap

The goal in education should be to prepare students for the opportunities of the future. It is not known what these opportunities will be exactly, but by teaching and encouraging students to create, collaborate, and communicate we can insure they have the skills to embrace those opportunities when they arise in the future. But many students are at a disadvantage because of both their past and their present.

Most of the students that one associates with the negative consequences of the Achievement Gap are hit the hardest by the "Opportunity Gap." The Opportunity Gap is the manner in which race, ethnicity, socioeconomic status, English proficiency, community wealth, familial situations, or other factors can contribute to lower educational aspirations, achievement, and attainment for students based on the opportunities, or lack thereof, they are afforded (Wells, Fox, and Cordova-Coba, 2016).

It is not hard to see how the financial status, race, or residency of a student can limit the opportunities that they have been exposed to. For example, if a student has been raised in poverty, they may not have had the opportunity to take family vacations. Now compare that to the experiences of a student whose family took a family vacation to Philadelphia, Pennsylvania. When these two students later sit in an eighth grade Social Studies class and the teacher begins talking about the Revolutionary War and the Declaration of Independence, which student begins with a better understanding? Which students has a more accurate picture as to what Independence Mall looks like and entails?

The "opportunity to learn – the necessary resources, the curriculum opportunities, the quality teachers – that affluent students have, is what determines what people can do in life" (Darling-Hammond, 2015). It is obvious to see how the lack of opportunity that some students suffer has a tremendous effect on how well they do in school and in life. Students also learn from each other and can grow from the opportunities that their peers "share" with them. Students from historically disadvantaged families have just a 51 percent "opportunity to learn" when compared to White students (The Schott Foundation, 2016).

The "Opportunity Gap" can take many forms. A minority student may experience prejudice that denies equitable access to learning opportunities, that is, advanced/accelerated courses, high school graduation rates, college acceptance rates, and so on. Students raised in non-English-speaking households can be at a disadvantage as they miss out on opportunities due to language barriers. Students living in single-parent households may not receive the same level of support or guidance as those in two-parent households.

The students affected by the "Opportunity Gap" because of past and present circumstances will most likely miss out on future opportunities as well. If a student grows up in a low-income household where education was never a priority or, worse yet, thought of as a nuisance and in turn was never exposed to those peers who value it, how are they going to be ready for or even realize those new opportunities that arise? If they never saw a classmate aspire for or achieve something more, why would that student believe they could do so? High school was just something they had to do and college was something that those other people did.

Students who lack "middle-class" cultural exposure and capital or wealth and who have limited parental involvement are likely to have lower academic achievement than their better-resourced peers. The lack of childhood opportunities undoubtedly limits future success (Lareau, 1987). Yes, some are able to overcome this lack of opportunity, but the overwhelming majority do not.

Unfortunately, some leaders and educators may even resort to throwing up their hands and/or stop trying to help "those students." It is clear that racial and economic isolation and/or abandonment "deprives children of color of what are sometimes obliquely called networks of opportunity" (Stancil,

2018). The result impacts the psychological dimension of education for these students causing significant symbolic loss that can have far-reaching consequences.

The Confidence Gap

Looking at those that the general population often considers "successful," one of the characteristics they each seem to possess is confidence. Confidence in their ability, potential, and likelihood of being successful. The NFL or NBA star athlete, the powerful politician, the business tycoon, a favorite actor or musician, all have an air of confidence about them. Some may even have too much confidence and border on the side of cockiness. But they have it; they have confidence. They believe in themselves and that they can not only get the job done, but also get it done better than anyone else.

There has been a great deal of research regarding the "Confidence Gap" when it comes to the difference in men and women in leadership roles and success. Those same principles that make the Confidence Gap a real issue between men and women apply when it comes to students as well. A lack of confidence comes from within but is often garnered by a student's surroundings and environment. Students can lack confidence because of a fear that they will be judged to have traits that are associated with negative stereotypes of their race, gender, or ethnic group. This fear can cause a form of "toxic stress" (Steele, 1998). Confidence undoubtedly plays a part in the success of our students. Especially, the lack of confidence that some of our female, minority, and low-income students possess (Letourneau, et al, 2020).

If a young girl constantly hears that girls are not good at math or girls cannot do this or that, then is it any surprise that she may "give up" when it comes to math or not go into certain fields as an adult? If a young Latino boy living in poverty hears that good grades or college is something that "they" do and not "us," is there any amazement the same student does not even have college on his radar as a future goal? For many students this "Confidence Gap" takes away possibilities before they even know they exist. Students fear that they will do poorly and "confirm" the stereotypes of inferior intellectual ability. As a result, these students perform at levels below their ability and a self-fulfilling prophecy begins.

Students in this situation are now more focused on dealing with this continual stress and learning how to respond to it than they are on learning literacy or math. Some "learn" to deal with this stress by not trying – "I don't care about this stuff. Grades don't matter. Good grades are for nerds" – while others never truly develop any strategies or coping mechanisms. Poverty and exclusion can crush hope.

The Honesty Gap

The "Honesty Gap" has very little to do with a lack of "honesty" within students, but rather a lack of honesty within adults that some display and then allow to affect the achievement of students. There are simply implicit biases (to be discussed in more detail later in this chapter) that cause some adults, who are often unaware and do so unintentionally, to view some students as less capable than others.

The Honesty Gap has to do with a lack of self-reflection by those in education regarding how their biases and preconceived perceptions of students can limit those very students' success and achievement levels. The Honesty Gap can steal future opportunities from students, causing the students to "live up" to the low expectations of others.

Research and experts agree that it is the teacher that matters the most in regards to achievement (Wong et al., 2014). It is the teacher who creates the environment to learn and to succeed. Wong (2014) highlights a study comparing low- and high-achieving elementary students in New York City that found that teacher effectiveness and qualifications accounted for 90 percent of the variation between the "best and worst" students.

Students, generally, strive to make their teachers and other adults proud and want to live up to their expectations. According to Slack (2003), the most important factor in a child's level of achievement is the teacher. An ineffective teacher can affect student learning for years, but two ineffective teachers in subsequent years can damage a student's entire academic career. Thus, a teacher's perceptions of his/her students, and any biases, play a huge role in how the students are treated and how they see themselves.

Unfortunately, it is not uncommon to hear a parent or teacher when discussing "at-risk students" say something along the lines of "our students can't," or "they don't want to do well," or "those students," and so on. If the adults do not honestly believe that a child can achieve greatness, then how can one expect a nine-year-old Black boy living in poverty to believe that he can do well in class, in school, or in life?

Everyone has past experiences that result in varied levels and forms of bias. The key is, through some self-examination and reflection, to be honest with oneself so that one can limit how these biases affect viewpoints, expectations, teaching, and, more importantly, students.

This lack of honesty affects not only how children and/or students are treated but also what is expected from them. It eventually affects what students expect of themselves. When the teacher gives an assignment that is at an easier level, but tells the students that it is a hard assignment, the students develop a warped sense of reality. Their internal expectation soon matches that of the teacher; the same teacher who does not expect or think much of them to begin with.

The Mirror

One of the most important uses of a leader's time is to take the time to "pause" and reflect. Taking the time to reflect is taking the time to learn. As Gibbs (1988) states, "It is not sufficient to have an experience in order to learn. Without reflection on this experience, it may be quickly forgotten or its learning potential lost." The ability to truly examine their thoughts, core beliefs, past words, and actions can allow a leader to grow and help transform their environments to ones that can attain and sustain success for all members. Fleming (2014) goes on to say that this "insight into our thoughts" is the key to high achievement no matter the venue or environment. But for a school leader to be successful, it cannot stop with just reflection. There must be action.

Reflective practice is that action for effective education leaders (Sergiovanni, 1987). Through reflective practice leaders begin by self-assessing their leadership. They look for learning points (akin to teachable moments) within a situation to enhance their leadership. They take the time to truly evaluate their action to identify their deficits and learning needs to then develop action plans to address them. As a result, leaders change or modify their practice in response to a problem. This is an ongoing, continuous learning cycle of monitoring and adjusting their leadership practice.

A leader involved in reflective practice will follow its core principles as they grow and their leadership evolves. They understand that learning is an active process and that it must acknowledge and build upon prior experiences. These leaders remember that they can learn something from every situation or experience because learners construct knowledge through experience. Yes, having a great role model or mentor can be very powerful for a leader, but sometimes leaders can learn just as much by watching what NOT to do. The final core principle of reflective practice is that learning is often more effective when it is collaborative.

Regardless of the topic or concern, reflective practice is a strategy that all leaders should follow. The benefits are numerous, not just for the leaders, but for the school/district as an entirety. But when one considers the complexities and nuances surrounding the topics addressed in this text, reflective practice is a must. As a leader incorporates reflective practice principles and concepts in regards to equity, they must begin by examining the concept of, and their own, implicit bias.

Pritlove et al. (2019) state that implicit bias rests on the belief that people act on the basis of internalized schemas of which they are often unaware and thus can, and often do, engage in discriminatory behaviors without conscious intent. The experiences, exposures, and teachings of an individual's past allow the brain to notice patterns and make "connections" and decisions in a fraction of a second. But the same thought processes that help individuals make smart decisions can also make them biased. This tendency for stereotype-confirming thoughts to pass spontaneously through our minds is what psychologists call implicit bias. It sets people up to overgeneralize, sometimes leading to discrimination even when people feel they are being fair (Payne, Niemi, and Doris, 2018).

First and foremost, everyone is subject to implicit biases. Some are harmless. If one is asked who their favorite sports team is, the answer is most often an example of an implicit bias. There are some subconscious reasons for the answer – the team they live closest too, the fond memories (or not so fond depending on who the team is) of watching games with their family, and so on. Rarely is there a well-thought-out logical reason for the fandom. Their favorite team is their favorite team and that's it.

Obviously, though, there are numerous examples of where implicit bias can be a "bad" thing, a very bad thing. If past experiences and examples (television shows, school examples/lessons, books, stories, etc.) are that woman are "less than" men, not capable of doing "executive"-type jobs, or should be at home with their children, the brain's subconscious decisions and patterns will limit who will be hired and for what position. Even without "meaning" to do harm, the harm has been done.

As a side note, unfortunately some will take the approach that "implicit" bias means that they are not thinking about these biases and that, as a result, they cannot do anything about them. For that reason, this author will often refer to implicit bias as "personal bias." It is important to take action and accept responsibility for one's personal actions and the harm they may cause. But in an effort to highlight other resources and supports, this text will continue to use the implicit bias terminology.

The same way the brain noticed patterns and made connections from past experiences and knowledge to reinforce stereotypes, it can "relearn" new patterns to eliminate negative implicit biases. The key is that as a leader, one must stop and reflect on why or what one's initial thoughts and actions are and what they are "saying." When the principal examines the discipline records for the school or grade level, they must ask: "[W]hy" is there such a disproportionate number of Black students receiving certain consequences as compared to others? Why do some students get warnings and others detentions? Why do certain parents cause a sense of anxiety, fear, or annoyance when they call or come into school, whereas others are welcomed even though they often appear with a list of "things they need you to check on"?

It is just as important, and possibly more so, to examine these same implicit biases outside of school (most individuals "try" a little harder when they are at work because they "know" they should):

- Who do you sit with (or not sit with) in a room full of strangers?
- Do you always clutch your purse a little tighter or put your hand in your pocket to check your wallet when anyone stands next to you in the elevator or just when certain people do?
- Are certain music or TV channels automatically not your "type" even before you listen or watch?
- If asked to picture a scientist in your head and then asked to describe the picture that is in your head, would you begin by saying "He looks . . ."?

It is vital to realize that to have these thoughts or to have implicit biases does not make one a racist or evil or even a "bad" person. As stated previously everyone has implicit biases. What it simply means is that one has "stuff" doing on inside that needs to be examined. What it means is that one has picked up messages and things along the way that need to be addressed and "re-thunk." It means that these "issues" are determining the thoughts, actions, and reactions of leadership in schools, and in society as a whole. If leaders take the time and make the effort, they can relearn and correct these biases. To reimagine and repurpose some thoughts of Fullan for the purposes of the discussion here, **relearning is the work**.

To move past implicit biases, reflective practice and conscious effort are needed. Leadership must ask the why and then take action to correct the deficit thought processes at work. In the words of Maya Angelou, "We are only as blind as we want to be."

34

The excuse that "I didn't mean it that way" or blaming others "for being too sensitive" and "reading too much" into things is unacceptable. To get "better" in this area, a leader must truly want go get better. They need to want to understand – to understand how others feel and the ramifications of their actions and words. A leader needs to develop a sense of empathy for all involved to begin to know better. Once this is achieved, they can be held accountable to the old saying – "If you know better, DO better."

The Power of Diversity

The importance of diversity and the inclusion of numerous backgrounds, perspectives, and ideas is understood and valued across various levels of society. From the business perspective, a diverse workforce is a reflection of a changing global society. Diverse teams bring high value to businesses. Respecting individual differences benefits the workplace by creating a competitive edge, including increasing work productivity, creativity, staff morale, market share, and the image of the organization (Carr-Ruffino, 2013). The same is true in education.

Future leaders are expected to not just welcome diversity, but also to embrace it. It is natural that the value of diversity transfers into the world of education. The research is overwhelming.

According to the US Department of Education:

> A growing body of research shows that diversity in schools and communities can be a powerful lever leading to positive outcomes in school and in life. Racial and

socioeconomic diversity benefits communities, schools, and children from all backgrounds. Today's students need to be prepared to succeed with a more diverse and more global workforce than ever before. Research has shown that more diverse organizations make better decisions with better results. The effects of socioeconomic diversity can be especially powerful for students from low-income families, who, historically, often have not had equal access. (www .ed.gov/diversity-opportunity)

A diverse student population (by race, ethnicity, socioeconomic status, special education, ELL, and so on) directly impacts student performance. Working in a diverse educational setting enables students to concentrate and push themselves further – students work better in diverse environments (Henson and Eller, 1999). School integration and student diversity positively relate to academic accomplishment for students of all groups (Smith, 2017). This leads to an increased cultural awareness, stronger critical thinking skills, and increased creativity, better preparing students for adulthood (Kite and Clark, 2021). Having exposure to different and divergent perspectives leads to positive learning outcomes and can have long-lasting benefits well past formal education and impact future success.

It is important to highlight the fact that students feel safer in school and in life (present and in the future) when they are educated in diverse settings (Graham, 2018). In turn, students are able to learn about and from their peers and their different cultures and backgrounds. This allows them to have a greater sense of comfort with said differences. These students typically are more willing to listen respectfully to different viewpoints, rather than mock, scorn, or fear the unfamiliar. Students also become more comfortable with themselves, leading to a deeper sense of safety.

A study done by researchers at the University of California, Los Angles (UCLA) and the University of Groningen in the Netherlands expounds upon the importance of diversity for students. The study finds that friendships across ethnic and socioeconomic lines help protect youths from feeling vulnerable, making them less lonely and safer (Juvonen, Kogachi, and Graham, 2018). The students who reported these friendships also felt less victimized. According to Graham, "students benefit when they have the opportunity for cross-ethnic and class contact" (Graham, 2018).

Even with all the research and data that shows the benefits of diversity, many leaders and educators are afraid and ill-prepared to even discuss the topic or work toward equity for all. In an Ed Week (2020) survey, 82 percent of district leaders, principals, and teachers received no anti-racist or in-depth equity training. In addition, 59 percent stated they lacked the resources to support the implementation of a curriculum based in equity and anti-racist principles.

In a separate study conducted by the American School Superintendent Association (Decennial Study, 2020), only 21 percent of superintendents felt prepared to have conversations regarding race and equity even though 90 percent rated the importance of such conversations as very high. Leaders cannot back away from this challenge. They must address it head on. They have the power to influence equity issues and concerns positively. They can establish and influence cultures to help reduce and eliminate conflicts as they create an institutional multiplier effect which can more easily influence practice beyond their institutions (Miller, 2001).

In Friere's seminal work *Pedagogy of the Oppressed* (1970, p. 34), he states, "education either functions as an instrument which is used to facilitate the integration of the younger generation into the logic of the present system and bring about conformity or to become the practice of freedom, the means by which men and women deal critically and creatively with reality and discover how to participate in the transformation of their world." It is the responsibility of education leaders to help facilitate the latter.

As difficult as it may be to begin to engage in what Linton and Singleton refer to as Courageous Conversations, leaders must begin that process. While it is true that some may resist (and will undoubtedly be vocal about this resistance), a Pew Research Center survey (2019) shows that the majority of your colleagues are comfortable with these conversations and welcome them. The study reported that 77 percent of Black adults, 74 percent of White adults, 70 percent of Asian adults, and 62 percent of Hispanic adults felt comfortable engaging in conversations concerning race and equity.

It is vital that leaders, in the words of Dugan (2017), "turn our gaze inward" and look at themselves and the structures they oversee. Self-reflection and examination of internal policies (both written and unwritten) are key. There must be a commitment by leaders to make those who are invisible, visible. Leadership can no longer hide behind the feeling of discomfort. There is no change without a sense of "uncomfortability." Leadership must lean into discomfort, not shy away from a struggle. As Fredrick Douglass so proudly proclaimed, ". . .there is no progress without struggle."

Ally, Advocate, Activist

As one continues with this foundational footing, it is important to accept the fact that a leader cannot remain silent. As the Rev. Dr. Martin Luther King, Jr. stated, "The ultimate tragedy is not the oppression and cruelty of the bad people, but the silence over that by the good people."

It is not enough though to just point out issues or make the statement that things need to change. The time has come to offer and work toward solutions, not just to announce problems. As educational leaders evolve through their reflective practice and continued growth as researched practioners, their involvement and action can evolve as well through being an ally, advocate, and activist. An abridged overview of the terms is provided here.

Based upon past experience and learning, individuals can find themselves at either of the aspects of being an ally, advocate, or activist and will quite often move along these "levels" depending on the situation or topic. Like most things, this is an evolving process of growth and understanding.

Merriam-Webster defines an ally as "one that is associated with another as a helper: a person or group that provides assistance and support in an ongoing effort, activity, or struggle" (Merriam-Webster.com). An ally is someone who usually is not a target of oppression but still works to end it. To be an ally is to support.

As an ally, it is important to "shut up and listen" first though. Oftentimes well-meaning supporters begin speaking for and over the same people they are trying to help. Before an ally can speak up, they need to shut up and listen in order to truly learn about the issues. Even then, an ally must understand that their role is not to be the voice of others, but to support individuals as they find opportunity to use their own voice.

No matter the topic or situation, an educational leader should at the least be an ally. One of a leader's core responsibilities is to care for and support their students. You don't need to be gay to understand that the student "coming out" in a sometimes hostile and judgmental society is going to need support. Whether one agrees or not with their "lifestyle decision" (we could spend the entire book on just working through this choice of wording that many would choose to use here), at the least, a leader needs to support and be there for their student.

The next "level" on this fluid continuum is that of an advocate. An advocate is "one who supports or promotes the interests of a cause or group" (Merriam-Webster.com). An advocate is a person who publicly supports a change or policy. They speak and learn about social and political issues and as a result bring attention to injustices.

At this level a leader may speak out about the inherent biases of an advanced placement policy at the high school level or the disparity regarding the number of male and female students receiving special education classification. It is important to remember though that advocacy alone does not alter the conditions of the oppressed. It takes action.

An advocate aides the activist in their fight against that same injustice. Although different, both are necessary in order to create systemic change. The action or change must take place through activism.

An activist is defined as "one who advocates or practices activism: a person who uses or supports strong actions (such as public protests) in support of or opposition to one side of a controversial issue" (Merriam-Webster.com). An activist supports through strong actions. An activist is on the front lines. They are someone who supports the target of oppression when they are going out on a limb. They are active in and for the cause.

An activist, in the words of the late Senator John Lewis, is someone involved in "good trouble." An activist is an accomplice, collaborator, or "coconspirator." An activist will often cause "discomfort" to those who observe from the sidelines. But as previously stated, there is no change without discomfort. We need activists! We need them to talk to us, to push us, teach us, defy us, and contradict us.

In spite of the fact that many of America's heroes are celebrated for being activists – think the "fathers" of the country, Susan B. Anthony, the aforementioned Dr. King – in today's society being an activist often carries a negative connotation. But when it comes to one's response to injustice, Frederick Douglass (1857) said it best:

> Agitate. Agitate. Agitate. Those who profess to favor freedom and yet depreciate agitation, are people who want crops without ploughing the ground; they want rain without thunder and lightning; they want the ocean without the roar of its many waters. The struggle may be a moral one, or it

may be a physical one, or it may be both. But it must be a struggle. Power concedes nothing without a demand. It never did and it never will.

It is ironic that some will fight against the terms and concepts presented here. Many find it uncomfortable to take on the said roles of being an ally, advocate, and especially that of an activist. As an educator or as an administrator, these roles are "too much" for me or put me in too much of harm's way. Again, leadership – true leadership – is not easy. If the goal is to take the "easy way out," then the suggestion offered here is to "get out." Students and staff deserve leadership that will do the "right thing" even when it's not the easy thing.

But, back to the irony. Even though many in leadership positions shy away from these roles, isn't it exactly what is expected of the students in the schools they lead. For example, what are students told/taught to do when they see someone being picked on or being bullied?

1. At the least, be supportive of the student being "bullied." Go up to them to make sure they are OK. Listen to them and let them know you care. **Be an ally.**

2. Make sure you let those in authority know of the problem – tell the teacher what happened. It is not OK that this behavior is going on and it needs to end. **Be an advocate.**

3. Don't just stand there and let it happen – stop it! Get others to help stop it. Let the "bully" know this is not acceptable and that "we" will not allow it to continue. **Be an activist.**

What "Category" Are You?

The work ahead is not easy. Just "mastering" (as if you ever could really master this type of work) the foundations discussed in this chapter will be a continuous process of reflection, learning, and growth. Additional theories and knowledge to assist in that process will be presented in Chapter 9 for use in the journey to become a researched practioner. Before delving into the case studies though, let's briefly explore the four categories of people leaders will encounter as they initiate this work.

First, there will be people who know, understand, and want to help. They see the injustice and want to be part of the solution. Some may already know more about the struggle than the educational leader beginning their work in this arena. They do not see that as an issue though as they recognize that everyone has room for growth. These activists will fight with the leader (and against the leader if need be) to make things better for all students.

Next, there is that group of individuals who recognize that there may be some injustices, but rather than reject them, they embrace them. "This is the way it is and those people don't deserve anything better." It is true that this may be a small portion of the group (although unfortunately it is probably a larger portion than anyone wants to accept), but a leader must acknowledge that this group does exist. It must not stop the leader from doing the right thing, but they must remember that this group is always there.

The remaining groups or categories are the most vital. There is a group of people who just "don't know."

Based on their surroundings and experiences, they honestly don't know or see the injustices around them. This does not make them bad people. In fact, once they become aware of injustice, they are often appalled and want to work to make things right – an ally. With increased knowledge, patience, and support, this group will become a driving force for justice.

Finally, there is a group of individuals (teachers, administrators, board members, parents, etc.) who "don't know AND don't want to know." All people (or at least 99 percent of people) like to think of themselves as good people. They care about others and do what is right, in their minds. They want to be able to look in the mirror and feel good about the kind of person they see.

This last group don't know about the injustices that others speak of and refuses to learn or even consider them. They make comments like

- "I've never seen anything like that."
- "Everyone here gets along; we don't have those issues."
- "None of my students feel that way because they have never brought it to my attention."

They "don't know and they don't want to know." In their minds, they know that "good" people would do something if someone was being treated unfairly or unjustly. Good people would change things. They don't want to know because if they actually knew about the issues and acknowledged the issues, then they would either need to take action and make a change or they would have to accept that the person they see in the mirror may not be the good person they aspire to be. Rather than take action, they happily continue with the facade and pull the veil of alternative existence (Du Bois) to live their lives of "goodness" where nothing is wrong. This is the most important group to reach and the most dangerous if not reached.

Leadership is not easy, and to be "good" at it, it takes much more than a degree, certification, or even the title or name on the door. In the same way that just because someone has a driver's license, it doesn't make them an explorer, just because someone has the title of supervisor, principal, or superintendent, it doesn't make them an educational **leader**. True leadership takes work and is ever evolving. The hope is that the foundation given here paired with the following case studies can assist leaders in an exercise of reflection, learning, and growth regarding understanding the role of equity in education settings.

So, let's begin with the case studies. Similar to the strategies you were taught during your undergraduate teacher education training regarding beginning a test with an "easy" question, we will begin with a somewhat "easy" case study. (Not that any of these scenarios are easy. Remember to dig down past the surface to really examine the issues and injustices that may exist.)

"Should I Stay (Away) or Should I Go?" – PRIDE Parade Case Study

Dr. Laura Taylor is relatively new (beginning her second year) to the position of superintendent in the Wayne School District. Like most school districts, Wayne has its share of "issues," but overall she is very happy in Wayne and in the position of superintendent. Wayne is Dr. Taylor's first superintendency after twelve years of serving as a principal in two separate districts and several unsuccessful attempts at landing a superintendent position elsewhere.

Wayne is relatively close to her home (the next town over) and her family has embraced Wayne, attending numerous events and becoming a visible part of the community. They attend a local church where Dr. Taylor's husband serves on several committees. Dr. Taylor is very involved in the area's Fellowship of Christian Athletes (FCA) organization that serves Wayne and the four neighboring communities as well.

A group of community members have organized a "PRIDE" parade to take place in town and have gotten a large amount of press and feedback – some good and some not so good – regarding it. The stated goal of the group is to "Show support for ALL and to develop a sense of inclusion, understanding, and hope for Wayne." As the date approaches, more and more students and groups have become engaged in the process and will be participating in the parade. In addition, numerous staff members and even the teacher's association leadership will be taking part in the parade.

The opening of the parade will include remarks by the mayor, local chamber of commerce leadership, and the organizers of the event. The lead organizer, Ms. Shoemaker (a parent of two Wayne students), has asked Dr. Taylor to be a part of the opening ceremony and to offer a few comments.

Dr. Taylor is very hesitant about accepting the invitation. She knows that not everyone in the community supports the "PRIDE" parade. She knows that it would not go over well with her church or the FCA group as several members of both have already spoken out against "gay and lesbian lifestyles." In addition, she's not sure how it would be received by her School Board. Dr. Taylor really doesn't want to "rock the boat" and wishes Ms. Shoemaker had never invited her to take part in the parade.

In her mind she keeps asking, "Should I stay away or should I go?"

Background Regarding Wayne

Wayne is a "middle-class" suburban school district. The district does relatively well on the state assessments and the typical standardized tests administered. Out of the twenty-four school districts in the county, it usually ranks in the top one-third – Wayne was ranked as #7 this past year.

Student Demographics

Total students (P–12) – 5,800

71 percent White

14 percent Asian

9 percent Black

6 percent Latinx

19 percent free/reduced lunch

21 percent special education classification

68 percent of graduating seniors attend four-year colleges/ universities

Staff Demographics

40 percent of staff members have four or less years in the district

31 percent of staff members have twenty or more years in the district

95 percent White

2 percent Black

2 percent Asian

1 percent Latinx

The city of Wayne has a population of 17,250 and has seen an increase of new residents to the area. The proximity of Wayne to a large metropolitan city has made it a desirable location to those who work in the city. An aging population of "Waynies" has begun to move out of town as they retire and opened the door to "newbies." The average home is assessed at $310,000 and when a house goes up for sale it usually ends in a bidding war (for comparison purposes, the average price for a house in this state is $229,500). Houses rarely last more than a week or two on the market before they are sold.

Downtown Wayne has undergone as "revitalization and rebirth" over the last two to three years with the addition of new high-end shops, antique stores, and restaurants. Downtown Wayne is bustling with activity, especially over the weekends with both locals and out-of-town consumers flooding the streets. On a nice spring or summer evening, Downtown Wayne is the place to be.

Guiding Questions

1. Does it matter that this is a community event and not a school event?
2. Should Dr. Taylor consult with anyone in particular regarding her decision?
3. What if the event was for a different "cause"? How would Dr. Taylor proceed? For example, what if this were a parade/event remembering the Holocaust? Black Lives Matter? Equal Pay for Women?
4. By attending, who would Dr. Taylor be supporting? Who would she be "offending"?
5. Do Dr. Taylor's "beliefs" matter?

Please take the time to truly consider the situation and how you (as Dr. Taylor) might address the circumstances presented. You may use the Case Study Analysis Protocol sheet (Figure 3.1) that follows to help you work through the steps. Once you have completed your analysis of how you might proceed (and possible discussion), take a look at the "So,

What Happened?" section to see how the scenario actually played out (but don't peek!!!!). The "So What Happened?" section is not meant to assess or judge any decisions or the individuals involved; it is just a recounting of what actually happened in the scenarios.

READ

Critically read through the entire Case Study and then go back and re-read it. Make notes and/or highlight important facts or issues to be addressed. Define the problems that need to be addressed.

REMOVE

Once the READ phase is complete, REMOVE yourself from the situation. Take a break from the Case Study – and then contemplate…

RESTATE

With a clear mind, go back and RESTATE or summarize the Case Study as if explaining it to a trusted colleague or peer. Focus on and share the pertinent facts. Explain and elaborate on what the "problems" (or "possibilities") are.
Who are the victims? Are there any "unintentional" victims?

REMEDIES

Begin to make a list of possible remedies or courses of action. Do not stop with the first or best "solution". Even if, at first blush the solution appears to be "not a great choice" include it on your list. Truly brainstorm.

How would each be implemented? Who would be involved? Describe the steps that would be taken

RESPOND

Respond to the Case Study by selecting the best possible solution. It is vital to not only explain the solution but to also explain the "why" behind that solution. Elaborate on who the solution helps and how it addresses the various issues (both at the surface and below).

Identify and discuss any possible issues or pitfalls.

Figure 3.1 The 5R Case Study Analysis Protocol

So, What Happened?

Professionally, Dr. Taylor was truly concerned with the response of those in the community that may not support the "PRIDE Parade." Would her participation show support for a cause she did not feel as though she had the **permission** to support? She was also deeply concerned from a personal perspective. What would the ramifications for supporting the parade be with her church, with her volunteer organization (FCA), and even with her husband and other family members?

Dr. Taylor originally reached out to ask for help with figuring out a way to decline the invitation without upsetting those involved while at the same time explaining why she could not participate and hoping for my validation of her refusal. The consultation and discussion that followed never involved directing her what to do or what not to do. It focused completely on why she wanted to make sure she didn't offend the organizers.

She explained that even though she didn't think she had "permission to support this cause and represent the district in this way" (her wording), she didn't want those involved (especially students and staff) to feel as though she didn't care about them or their feelings. She wanted to show empathy. The discussion turned into a pseudo counseling session to work through some of her feelings, "beliefs," and biases. She was truly perplexed with what to do and how to show a form of support that she was comfortable with.

Eventually, she got to the point where she stated that she could not speak at the event, but still wanted to support her students and their "voices." She (with some slight guidance) decided that she would attend the parade and watch along the parade route through town. This way she could still support her students (and staff) without taking a lead by speaking. She informed the organizers that she did not want to speak during the opening ceremonies as the event shouldn't focus on her and suggested that a student leader instead speak in her place.

The parade went off without a hitch and was very well attended. For the most part, Dr. Taylor avoided the negative response she feared from both sides of the cause. She did receive two or three emails/phone calls from those who thought she should have done more as well as those who thought she should not have attended at all though. In our follow-up discussion, we discussed how, as a leader, there is always someone who is not happy with you. As a matter of fact, if everyone is happy with you, then you are probably doing something wrong.

4

"Only the Few, the Proud,
the Gifted . . .": Gifted and Talented
Case Study

At the elementary school level in the Goshen School District, all third grade students take a standardized test to measure their "IQ." That data is then used to determine who is placed into the Gifted and Talented (G&T) program. The G&T program at Goshen is highly regarded and seen as a badge of accomplishment by many in the community. Students in the G&T program have access to additional learning activities and events. The teachers associated with the G&T program receive additional training and support (including financial support) for the associated activities.

Once students reach the middle school level, students from G&T programs are then automatically placed in "Accelerated" Math and/or ELA based on teacher recommendations. As these same students continue to Goshen High School, they are again eligible for "Honors" and "AP" courses based upon teacher and counselor recommendations.

At a recent Board of Education meeting, a parent (Marisol Cantina) complained about these "unfair" practices and how they limit the opportunities for students. In particular, she said that this selective process hurts some Latinx students, and other students who may be learning English as a second language. These students are then boxed out from being included in future "advanced" coursework largely based upon their elementary education placements. Ms. Cantina stated that it may be true that some students are able to overcome these obstacles (her son Vahid would be an example as he is enrolled in three AP courses at Goshen High School), but that this is the exception rather than the rule. She is concerned about the students who may not have as much support as her children do. Some parents may not even understand that they can fight and advocate for their child's inclusion in the accelerated or advanced classes.

After Ms. Cantina's comments, one of the Board of Education members asked the table of administrators at the meeting for their thoughts and/or response. The principal at Goshen High School stated that he was "just following what we have always done." No other administrator offered a response.

The Board of Education has now directed the super-intendent, Dr. Alfred Hilwig, to look into the allegations and to report back at next month's meeting. Dr. Hilwig has been the superintendent in the district for seven years. Prior to that, he was the principal at one of the middle schools in Goshen for eight years and a teacher in the district for twelve years.

Background Regarding Goshen Township

Goshen Township is a rural upper-middle-class school dis-trict. The district takes pride in the fact that many of the graduating seniors move on to highly regarded colleges and universities.

Student Demographics

Total students (P–12) – 2,500
75 percent White
4 percent Asian
12 percent Black
9 percent Latinx
15 percent free/reduced lunch
17 percent special education classification
60 percent of graduating seniors attend four-year colleges/
  universities

Staff Demographics

11 percent of staff members have four or less years in the
  district
55 percent of staff members have twenty or more years in the
  district
97 percent White
2 percent Black
0 percent Asian
1 percent Latinx

Gifted and Talented Demographics

94 percent of G&T students are White
4 percent of G&T students are Asian
1 percent of G&T students are Black
1 percent of G&T students are Latinx

100 percent of staff associated with G&T are White and have more than twenty-five years of experience in district

Goshen Township has a population of 4,189 in a beautiful rural setting. It has a strong farming past and is a picturesque history-filled community. Several houses date back to the early 1700s. The population has remained fairly consistent over the past thirty years. People rarely move out of Goshen Township. It is even rarer for new families to move in.

If you were to look through school yearbooks over the years, several family names would be mainstays no matter the year or decade. There is definitely "old money" in Goshen Township held by a few prominent families. These same families also hold prominent positions in both business and elected office in the township.

Guiding Questions

1. Is the current G&T "selection process" fair and equitable?
2. Who does the current process help (if anyone)? Who does it harm (if anyone)?
3. Who should Dr. Hilwig speak/meet with concerning the G&T process?
4. Is this only a G&T issue, or is it bigger (hint: it's always bigger)?
5. In general, what is the purpose of G&T at the elementary level? Who (which students) does this "goal" pertain to?

Please take the time to truly consider the situation and how you might address the circumstances presented. You may use the Case Study Analysis Protocol sheet

(Figure 4.1) that follows to help you work through the steps. Once you have completed your analysis of how you (as Dr. Hilwig) might proceed (and possible discussion), take a look at the "So, What Happened?" section to see how the scenario actually played out (but don't peek!!!!). The "So What Happened?" section is not meant to assess or judge any decisions or the individuals involved, it is just a recounting of what actually happened in the scenarios.

READ

Critically read through the entire Case Study and then go back and re-read it. Make notes and/or highlight important facts or issues to be addressed. Define the problems that need to be addressed.

REMOVE

Once the READ phase is complete, REMOVE yourself from the situation. Take a break from the Case Study – and then contemplate…

RESTATE

With a clear mind, go back and RESTATE or summarize the Case Study as if explaining it to a trusted colleague or peer. Focus on and share the pertinent facts. Explain and elaborate on what the "problems" (or "possibilities") are.
Who are the victims? Are there any "unintentional" victims?

REMEDIES

Begin to make a list of possible remedies or courses of action. Do not stop with the first or best"solution". Even if, at first blush the solution appears to be "not a great choice" include it on your list. Truly brainstorm.

How would each be implemented? Who would be involved? Describe the steps that would be taken

RESPOND

Respond to the Case Study by selecting the best possible solution. It is vital to not only explain the solution but to also explain the "why" behind that solution. Elaborate on who the solution helps and how it addresses the various issues (both at the surface and below).

Identify and discuss any possible issues or pitfalls.

Figure 4.1 The 5R Case Study Analysis Protocol

So, What Happened?

Obviously, this situation is much more than just the G&T program. It revolves around tracking, access, and equity for all students, as well as staff in some regards (placements/teaching assignments, resources, etc.).

Research has shown that limiting student opportunity by placing students in tracks, especially at the early grades, negatively affects student growth and potential along racial and socioeconomic lines. Typically, the resulting "tracks" are racially homogenous, creating separate and far from equal learning environments and student outcomes. Eric Hanushek, a fellow at Hoover Institution at Stanford University, found that restricting the racial and socioeconomic exposure of students hurts all children (2013). Furthermore, Black students' test scores tend to go up when they are in integrated environments. White children's scores, meanwhile, are not negatively affected at all (Felton, 2017). Rucker Johnson, an economist at the University of California, Berkley, found that White students who attended integrated classes have measurably less racial prejudice and tend to live in more integrated neighborhoods as adults. Latino and Black students who attended integrated classes earn more as adults, live longer, healthier lives, and even pass down these benefits to their children (Felton, 2017).

Unfortunately, Dr. Hilwig did not "dig deeper" and only looked at the G&T selection process at the surface level. He spoke with his "lead" G&T teacher, Ms. Ragan, a thirty-four-year teaching veteran in the district. She told him how the "gifted" students needed this outlet. She stated that her G&T students discussed how they sometimes feel isolated in class –

some felt that their teachers always selected them for answers and that they were expected to be perfect, while others felt that their teachers never selected them because they wanted to give other students a chance. Ms. Ragan stated that her students needed this space to just be themselves and not feel isolated and alone. She also expressed that it would be a disservice to "slow things down" by allowing other students to be involved if they didn't "deserve" it.

Dr. Hilwig then spoke to a parent of a former G&T student (who also happened to be a Board of Education member), Mr. Stewart. Mr. Stewart spoke about how his son excelled with the hands-on projects that he experienced in the G&T program. Mr. Stewart feels as though it was those experiences and connections (he specifically referred to a guest speaker who was an engineer) that led his son to major in engineering at college.

Dr. Hilwig never contacted Ms. Cantina to get any feedback from her.

What Dr. Hilwig (and Ms. Ragan and Mr. Stewart) missed is that all students deserve the benefits described by those involved in the G&T program. If the "advanced" students need a place to connect and to feel included, don't you think the other students could have the same needs? The hands-on projects meet the learning needs of many other students and are strategies typically suggested for students who may be struggling. And who needs a mentor or "inspiration" more than those students who may not be experiencing success routinely? (I know, I'm not supposed to be offering commentary or my thoughts here. Sorry, I just couldn't help myself! Besides, I didn't even get into IQ testing.)

So at the next Board of Education meeting, Dr. Hilwig reported that the G&T program is one of the district's most successful programs. He highlighted the colleges that G&T graduates have attended and awards they have won. He also highlighted the words of Ms. Ragan and Mr. Stewart, celebrating the success of the program as structured. He concluded his presentation by stating that the "IQ" test they use isn't biased and is used by many other districts. The Board of Education president thanked him for his presentation, and the meeting moved on with the agenda.

Once the meeting reached the "public comment" section of the agenda, Ms. Cantina expressed her displeasure with Dr. Hilwig's "presentation" and with the fact that he never even reached out to her for a meeting or to discuss her concerns. In her comments, she stated that "this is not over." And she was correct. The lack of respect from Dr. Hilwig and the district was not only felt by Ms. Cantina, but was just another example of a continuing theme that some parents felt when dealing with the school district. In the coming months more and more questions were asked surrounding equity practices in the district and more examples of "unfair" practices/decisions began to surface.

The district is currently involved in three different lawsuits regarding inequitable practices/policies and discrimination.

5

"Weird Book" – Book Censorship Case Study

Ms. Alvarez is in her third year of teaching and has spent her entire career thus far in the Red Banksville School District's only elementary school of 350 students. As part of the Red Banksville School District's second grade curriculum, Ms. Alvarez is teaching a unit on family structure and diversity. The unit discusses the various roles of family members and how the family unit can be different in various cultures. The unit also emphasizes that "no one family structure is better than another. It is important to remember that each person's family is important to them and that we should respect all kinds of families and people." There has been an emphasis in the district regarding cultural responsiveness by the new curriculum supervisor, Ms. Lolle, and this recently revised board-approved curriculum shows such. The resources section in the district's curriculum offers several stories for use with this unit. Ms. Alvarez picks an award-winning story about "Clyde's Family" and his two dads.

The story focuses around an eight-year-old boy, Clyde, and the daily interactions he and his family have in the town of Wilson. Clyde's family consists of himself, his adopted little sister, and his two dads. Ms. Alvarez reads the story during "story time" and the students are attentive and well behaved. After she finishes, the students discuss different types of family structures and are quick to share – one student points out that he lives with his dad and two sisters, another discusses how she lives with her grandparents, another with his mom, dad, and four sisters, and yet another shares that she lives with her two moms and brother. The students are all very respectful and actively engaged in the discussion. In Ms. Alvarez's opinion, the lesson turns out to be one of her better lessons of the year and she continues on with the rest of the day's lessons and assignments with a sense of accomplishment.

Ms. Alvarez begins the next day of school full of optimism and excitement for another productive day with her very energetic second grade students until she receives an email that morning from her principal, Mr. Mancini, stating that some parents have complained about her lesson and the reading of "that weird book" in class. The email is short and the tone is that of annoyance. In the email, Mr. Mancini informs her that she needs to be at a meeting immediately after school with him, and some of the parents, to explain. He also tells her to bring her lesson plans and the book with her to the meeting.

Background Regarding Red Banksville

The Red Banksville School District is a "small" suburban school district of 925 students and consists of one elementary, one middle, and one high school. Typically, once someone is hired in the district, they stay "for life." As such, the principals at each of the three schools are "lifers" and each has more than twenty years' experience in education, all occurring within the district. Mr. Mancini, the principal of the elementary school, runs a very "tight ship." Being the administrator with the most seniority (thirty-four years in the district and fifteen as principal of the elementary school), some believe there is some animosity between him and the central office as he was passed over by the Board of Education when the new superintendent was hired four years ago. Some also believe it didn't help matters that he was not asked to be the new curriculum supervisor last year, even though he never officially applied for the position.

Student Demographics

Total students (P–12) – 925
67 percent White
16 percent Black
12 percent Latinx
5 percent Asian
39 percent free/reduced lunch
29 percent special education classification

Staff Demographics

21 percent of staff members have four or less years in the district
52 percent of staff members have twenty or more years in the district
88 percent White
6 percent Black
5 percent Latinx
1 percent Asian

The borough of Red Banksville is a small suburban location approximately fifteen minutes away from the popular beach destinations of the area. It has a population of 3,700, which has remained fairly stagnant over the past forty years. During the summer months, the population explodes to over 12,000 due to summer homes and rentals.

Guiding Questions

1. Who might Ms. Alvarez speak to (or consult with) prior to the meeting with Mr. Mancini and the parents?
2. How else might Mr. Mancini have initially responded to the parent complaints instead of immediately setting up a meeting with the parents and Ms. Alvarez?
3. Is this an example of any greater issues (of course it is)? If so, what?
4. Does anyone *deserve* a "heads up" regarding this situation?
5. What role does "power" (its use and possible "abuse") play in this scenario?

Please take the time to truly consider the situation and how you might address the circumstances presented. You may use the Case Study Analysis Protocol sheet (Figure 5.1) that follows to help you work through the steps. Once you have completed your analysis of how you (as Ms. Alvarez AND then as Mr. Mancini) might proceed (and possible discussion), take a look at the "So, What Happened?" section to see how the scenario actually played out (but don't peek!!!!). The "So What Happened?" section is not meant to assess or judge any decisions or the individuals involved, it is just a recounting of what actually happened in the scenarios.

READ

Critically read through the entire Case Study and then go back and re-read it. Make notes and/or highlight important facts or issues to be addressed. Define the problems that need to be addressed.

REMOVE

Once the READ phase is complete, REMOVE yourself from the situation. Take a break from the Case Study – and then contemplate...

RESTATE

With a clear mind, go back and RESTATE or summarize the Case Study as if explaining it to a trusted colleague or peer. Focus on and share the pertinent facts. Explain and elaborate on what the "problems" (or "possibilities") are.
Who are the victims? Are there any "unintentional" victims?

REMEDIES

Begin to make a list of possible remedies or courses of action. Do not stop with the first or best "solution". Even if, at first blush the solution appears to be "not a great choice" include it on your list. Truly brainstorm.

How would each be implemented? Who would be involved? Describe the steps that would be taken

RESPOND

Respond to the Case Study by selecting the best possible solution. It is vital to not only explain the solution but to also explain the "why" behind that solution. Elaborate on who the solution helps and how it addresses the various issues (both at the surface and below).

Identify and discuss any possible issues or pitfalls.

Figure 5.1 The 5R Case Study Analysis Protocol

So, What Happened?

Ms. Alvarez spent the rest of the day "stressing" about her upcoming meeting at the end of the day with Mr. Manicini and the parents. She knew how Mr. Mancini had acted toward her and other staff in the past. He did not want any issues of any kind. "Don't rock the boat" was one of his often-used catch phrases. He had also been stern when speaking to teachers in the past, sometimes to the point of scolding and talking down to teachers as if they were children and he was the parent. She worried to the point where she was sick to her stomach.

She also wondered who the parents were that complained and who she would be meeting with. No one had reached out to her. She thought she had established good two-way communication with her parents. They often reached out to her to ask questions, discuss concerns, and to just check in through the various formats she offered – email, phone, SeeSaw app, and so on. Even though she tried to fight the urge, she found herself looking at each of her students through the day and wondering which one went home and complained to their parents about the lesson. Which one was the mole? It would be an understatement to say that this was not one of her best teaching days with her students. It was impossible for her to focus on her lessons or her students.

As the day ended, Ms. Alvarez tentatively made her way to Mr. Mancini's office for the meeting. Once there, she sat at one end of the large conference table in his office. Mr. Mancini sat at the other end of the table along with a gentleman that Ms. Alvarez did not quite recognize.

Mr. Manicini began the meeting by asking Ms. Alvarez, "Why did you read that weird book" to your students? As Ms. Alvarez attempted to answer, Mr. Mancini cut her off and began berating her for doing something that was so "completely inappropriate" and "stupid." This continued for approximately fifteen minutes.

Eventually, Ms. Alvarez was able to get out that the story is actually part of the second grade curriculum and is listed as a suggested resource. At that point, Mr. Mancini looked at the other gentleman in the room and said, "See, Charlie! This is because you guys hired that *girl* to be in charge of curriculum. I told you not to hire her!" It was then that Ms. Alvarez realized that the other gentleman at the table was Mr. Charles (Charlie) Kilinger, a longtime Board of Education member and friend of Mr. Mancini – not a parent of one of her students.

Toward the end of the meeting, Ms. Alvarez was finally able to get a word in and ask what parents had complained about the lesson. Mr. Mancini sternly responded that Mr. Kilinger had heard about the lesson and was very displeased. Mr. Mancini then told her that if she valued her job, she "better not use that book or teach a similar lesson again." He then dismissed her from his office.

A visibly upset and crying Ms. Alvarez exited the office and returned to her classroom. Soon afterward, Ms. Ledger (teacher association president) came into her room and asked her what had happened. Ms. Alvarez explained the entire situation and how she was treated. Ms. Ledger took notes and assured Ms. Alvarez that she did nothing wrong and that Mr. Mancini was not going to get away with this again!

It turned out that this was the third grievance of this type filed against Mr. Mancini that year. The superintendent had already placed Mr. Mancini on a Corrective Action Plan and there had already been several "incidents" between Mr. Mancini and the new curriculum supervisor, Ms. Lolle. At the end of the school year, the superintendent recommended withholding Mr. Mancini's salary increment, which the Board of Education approved.

This was also not the first complaint about Mr. Kilinger overstepping his bounds as a board member either. This time "ethics" charges were filed with the state noting this incident and several previous "inappropriate" actions. Before a final decision from the State Board of Ethics could be rendered, Mr. Kilinger decided not to run for reelection and gave up his seat on the board.

Ms. Alvarez remains in the district, but unfortunately has never used the story about "Clyde" and his two dads or taught a similar lesson again.

6

"Just Not a Good Fit" – Hiring
Practices Case Study

It is early July and Mr. Wilson is a member of the selection committee involved in the hiring of a new language arts teacher at Schmidt High School. The committee is made up of several members of the high school staff, including himself (a history teacher with three years of experience in the district), Ms. Moore (a language arts teacher with nine years of experience in the district), Mr. McAdams (a special education teacher with twelve years in the district), and Mr. Brown (the language arts department chair with twenty years of experience in the district). The committee's charge is to present the top two choices for the position to the principal.

The interview process for Schmidt High School involved several phases. After a review of resumes, the committee selected twelve candidates to come in for the first round. Here, each candidate participated in a short (fifteen- to twenty-minute) "get-to-know-you" interview. To assist with time, each committee member individually interviewed three separate candidates from the first round pool. Each committee member used a district-supplied set of questions. The first round pool of twelve candidates was then narrowed down to five candidates based upon the discussion of committee members and the scores from the rubric used for first round interviews in the district.

For round two, the candidates conducted sample lessons (to a group of students involved in one of the district's summer enrichment programs), which were observed by all four of the committee members. The candidates then participated in a second interview. The second interview was more involved and lasted approximately one hour. All of the committee members participated in this interview and took turns asking questions from the district's round two set of questions. The committee then met to discuss which two candidates should be presented to the principal.

As the discussion began, it was clear that two of the candidates would not move forward. They both did "poorly" during their sample lessons – one repeatedly spelled words incorrectly on the display panel, while the other candidate became visibly flustered when he lost his place during his lesson. So, it came down to three candidates for the two spots to move on.

The first of the remaining candidate had a score of 89 (out of 100) for the first round interview (conducted by Ms. Moore). She recently graduated college in May and was not overly involved in extra curricula activities – she stated she was "not really a sports or activity kinda girl." Her sample lesson went fairly well. The students were fairly engaged, but lost interest by the end of the lesson. The candidate is White.

The second remaining candidate had a score of 91 for the first round interview (conducted by Mr. Brown). He graduated college three years ago and has spent the last couple of years substituting in various districts. He was involved in student government in college and was a member of a fraternity (the same fraternity that Mr. Brown was a member of). Besides substitute teaching, he has also been a DJ for events and parties since graduation. By all accounts, his sample lesson went "OK." The students were fairly attentive, but several times during his lesson the candidate went off topic and began talking about music and sports with the students. This candidate is also White.

The third remaining candidate had a score of 95 for the first round interview (conducted by Mr. Wilson). She recently graduated college this past May and did her student teaching at a highly respected district in a neighboring community. While there, she was trained on the new language arts program that Schmidt High School will be implementing this schoolyear. Both at college and during her student teaching, the candidate was involved in numerous activities – National Honor Society, school newspaper, debate club, drama productions, yearbook, cross country/track and field, and so on. Based upon observation and student feedback (gathered from the "exit ticket" she used with her students to close the lesson), her lesson went very well. The students were actively engaged and even continued discussing her lesson as they left the room for their lunch. The candidate is Asian.

By the time the committee finished with the interviews and began the discussion on who should move forward, it was well past lunch. Ms. Moore began by saying she thought that any of the three remaining options would be "good with her" and that each would do "fine." She then said she had to leave to pick up her children from day camp. She quickly grabbed her belongings and left.

Mr. McAdams quickly added that he had to leave in a few minutes as well due to another commitment. He also stated that any of the remaining three would be fine with him. Mr. Wilson then offered his takeaways from the lessons and the interviews involving the three remaining finalists. He stated that the third candidate was his top choice "hands down," with candidate one as his backup.

Mr. Brown then thanked both Mr. McAdams and Mr. Wilson for "hanging in there" for such a long day. He stated he would be sending candidates one and two on to the principal, with candidate two as his top choice. Mr. McAdams replied, "Sounds good to me," and gathered his belongings and quickly exited the room. Mr. Wilson was quite surprised and asked, "What about the third candidate?" By this time, Mr. Brown had collected all of the notes and documentation from the committee. He looked across the table at Mr. Wilson and said, "She was nice and all, but she's just not a good fit for my Language Arts Department." With a sly smirk on his face, he then added, "Might be a different story if this was the Math Department."

Background Regarding Schmidt High School

Schmidt High School is a "working-class" high school, which in many regards is living in the past. It is not uncommon to hear staff members reminiscing about the "good old' days." The school has seen a constant decline in student population over the past fifteen years (at one time the school was home to over 1,800 students). The school building itself is in need of constant repair. There has been discussion recently regarding whether the school should even remain open or to consolidate it with another high school in the district.

Student Demographics

Total students (9–12) – 600
61 percent White
21 percent Latinx
15 percent Black
3 percent Asian
58 percent free/reduced lunch
34 percent special education classification
44 percent of graduating seniors attend four-year colleges/ universities

Staff Demographics

16 percent of staff members have four or less years in the district
61 percent of staff members have twenty or more years in the district
97 percent White
1 percent Black
1 percent Latinx

The surrounding area near Schmidt High School reflects some of the same issues of the school itself. There are many abandoned houses and buildings in the adjacent blocks to the school. The area once was home to a flourishing glass manufacturer. The company moved its headquarters fifteen years ago and then soon closed down the manufacturing facility in the neighborhood. When those jobs left, so did many of the residents and the prosperity that had once been the norm.

Guiding Questions

1. Discuss the hiring/interview process. Are there any good practices being followed? Are there any "not so good" practices being followed?
2. What are your thoughts regarding each of the committee members? Does this give you any additional insight into the overall culture of the school?
3. Does the principal share any "responsibility" in this situation?
4. Students were involved in this process, but were their voices "heard"? Valued?
5. What components of the Achievement Gap may be involved here?

Please take the time to truly consider the situation and how you might address the circumstances presented. You may use the Case Study Analysis Protocol sheet (Figure 6.1) that follows to help you work through the steps. Once you have completed your analysis of how you (as Mr. Wilson) might proceed (and possible discussion), take a look at the "So, What Happened?" section to see how the scenario actually played out (but don't peek!!!!). The "So What Happened?" section is not meant to assess or judge any decisions or the individuals involved, it is just a recounting of what actually happened in the scenarios.

READ

Critically read through the entire Case Study and then go back and re-read it. Make notes and/or highlight important facts or issues to be addressed. Define the problems that need to be addressed.

REMOVE

Once the READ phase is complete, REMOVE yourself from the situation. Take a break from the Case Study – and then contemplate...

RESTATE

With a clear mind, go back and RESTATE or summarize the Case Study as if explaining it to a trusted colleague or peer. Focus on and share the pertinent facts. Explain and elaborate on what the "problems" (or "possibilities") are.
Who are the victims? Are there any "unintentional" victims?

REMEDIES

Begin to make a list of possible remedies or courses of action. Do not stop with the first or best"solution". Even if, at first blush the solution appears to be "not a great choice" include it on your list. Truly brainstorm.

How would each be implemented? Who would be involved?
Describe the steps that would be taken

RESPOND

Respond to the Case Study by selecting the best possible solution. It is vital to not only explain the solution but to also explain the "why" behind that solution. Elaborate on who the solution helps and how it addresses the various issues (both at the surface and below).

Identify and discuss any possible issues or pitfalls.

Figure 6.1 The 5R Case Study Analysis Protocol

So, What Happened?

Mr. Wilson just could not get the comment (and smirk) from Mr. Brown out of his head. The next day, he went to the school and asked to speak to Mr. North (the principal) so that he could make him aware of the appalling comment and unprofessionalism displayed by Mr. Brown during the interview process. Unfortunately, Mr. North was not there. His secretary notified Mr. Wilson that Mr. North was out on vacation for the next week. Mr. Wilson left a message with the secretary and asked Mr. North to reach out to him once he returned.

Mr. Wilson also sent an email to Mr. North expressing the same and stating that he had major concerns regarding the hiring process for the new language arts teacher and the recommendation from the hiring committee chaired by Mr. Brown. In addition, Mr. Wilson sent an email to Mr. Brown expressing that he was uncomfortable with his recommendation and comment. After two days of not getting a response from Mr. Brown (or Mr. North), Mr. Wilson emailed the entire committee and let them know of his concerns. No one responded.

Two weeks went by and Mr. Wilson grew increasingly frustrated. After several more emails and even two phone calls (and leaving voicemails) to Mr. North, Mr. Wilson went to the school again in an attempt to voice his concerns to Mr. North. This time Mr. North was in the office, although he said he was leaving soon (it was 1:30 PM). Mr. Wilson asked him if he could speak to him and if he had gotten his messages about the hiring recommendation.

Mr. North informed him that he had gotten his messages and that he had two minutes.

Mr. Wilson explained the situation and his concerns. Mr. North replied, "I think you are overreacting, don't you? Besides, it doesn't really matter now because the teacher (Candidate two) was approved at the Board of Education meeting two days ago."

Mr. Wilson exclaimed, "What? Really? Why didn't you call me or respond to any of my messages or emails? You knew I had concerns about this."

Mr. North matter-of-factly responded, "Because I'm busy and now I'm leaving. Goodbye, Wilson."

Mr. Wilson was in shock and infuriated by the disrespect he felt Mr. North displayed toward him and the situation. He reached out to his teacher association representative to explain the situation. The rep listened, but offered no solution or course of action. He also shared the story with several of his colleagues who all listened, but did not seem to share his anger regarding the situation.

The following school year was a difficult one for Mr. Wilson. Everything seemed different. The colleagues he had worked so closely with during his time in the district were all "way too busy" when it came to having conversations with him. He was even left out of the group for the impromptu "Happy Hours" on Fridays after school. For the first three years in the district, all of his observations were "distinguished" and filled with glowing remarks of praise and accomplishment. This year, two of his observations were at the "basic" level and one was rated as "poor" – the "poor" observation was conducted by Mr. North.

In May, he was called into the office by Mr. North and given a letter stating that he would not be renewed for the next year. He was in shock. He asked Mr. North for the reason why, to which Mr. North responded, "You're just not a good fit."

Mr. Wilson subsequently contacted the state office of his teachers association and filed a wrongful termination lawsuit. Two years later the district settled with Mr. Wilson for an undisclosed amount. Mr. North has been reassigned to another position in the district.

7

"Must be the Music" – Hateful Language Case Study

Ms. Tyson is just finishing up a lesson in her Honors English III class. The students did a nice job of remaining engaged throughout the lesson and Ms. Tyson is pleased with how the lesson went, especially considering that next period is the Pep Rally for the big football game tonight. Ms. Tyson has been at Cheyney High School for seven years and she knows that the students often lose any semblance of focus during Pep Rally days. So, since things went well, Ms. Tyson gives the students the last seven to eight minutes of class time to relax and "talk quietly."

Within two minutes, a group of students in the back become loud and one of them, Stephanie, yells to Ms. Tyson, "Did you hear that? He can't say that! That's not right!!!" Ms. Tyson quickly stands up from behind her desk and walks to the back of the classroom. After she calms down everyone in the group, she asks Stephanie to explain what happened.

STEPHANIE: "James just said the N-word!!"
JAMES: "I was just singing a song! She needs to calm down and mind her own business . . . we sing that song in the locker room all the time at football practice. It gets us hyped for the game. . . . Everyone sings it and no one has

a problem with it. Not even the Black kids on the team complain about it!"

STEPHANIE: "That doesn't matter. ... I have a problem with it!"

JAMES: "Whatever! You're white like I am. ... You can't have a problem with it."

As the two students become louder and more upset, Ms. Tyson again calms everyone down. She has heard students singing the rap song in question before in the hallways and in the cafeteria. No one seemed to find it offensive, not even the Black students who she saw nearby. But Stephanie was obviously upset.

Ms. Tyson talks to the students some more and settles down Stephanie. She explains that words can absolutely cause harm and that everyone must be mindful of that fact. She reminds them of a project that they worked on last quarter on inclusiveness and poetry. Ms. Tyson informs James that since Stephanie is offended by the song, he should not sing it around her again and that he should respect her feelings. As the bell rings to report to the Pep Rally, James quickly replies, "OK" and the students left the classroom.

Ms. Tyson thinks to herself, "It never fails! Of course, it was Friday afternoon and a Pep Rally!" But, she has successfully and quickly resolved the situation (or so she thinks).

Stephanie, on the other hand, does not feel as though the situation was resolved. She quickly leaves Ms. Tyson's classroom and goes to the principal's office. She asks to speak to Mr. Lee. To her dismay, Mr. Lee is not available. He is in the gymnasium for the Pep Rally and is not available to talk to her. Stephanie informs the secretary that this is an "emergency" and is visibly upset. The secretary replies, "I'm sure it is an emergency, dear, but you'll have to get over it." The secretary then tells Stephanie that she will let Mr. Lee know on Monday that Stephanie stopped in and wanted to speak to him. She says, "He'll probably call you down later in the day on Monday." Stephanie leaves feeling frustrated but vows to come see him again first thing Monday morning.

Stephanie is even more enraged and her feelings of not letting things go more reinforced after the Pep Rally. As she walks past the locker room door to leave the building to go home, she hears the same particular rap song James was singing in class being loudly played from inside. She can even hear James singing the part with the N-word being stated repeatedly.

Background Regarding Cheyney High School

Cheyney High School is one of three high schools in the Southville School District. Southville as a whole is an upper-middle-class "above average" school district. Cheyney High School in particular is considered the "shining star" of the district and is considered one of the best high schools in the region. Students typically get accepted into prestigious colleges and universities across the country. Cheyney excels not only academically but also athletically. The school has won numerous conference and sectional titles in multiple sports over the past few years. For example, the girls basketball team won the state championship for their division last year. The football team has made the playoffs for three straight years.

Student Demographics

Total students (9–12) – 2,450
81 percent White
9 percent Black
5 percent Latinx
4 percent Asian
15 percent free/reduced lunch
29 percent special education classification
88 percent of graduating seniors attend four-year colleges/ universities

Staff Demographics

21 percent of staff members have four or less years in the district
34 percent of staff members have twenty or more years in the district
96 percent White
2 percent Black
1 percent Asian
1 percent Latinx

The city of Southville has a population of 17,250 and has seen a small increase of new residents to the area in recent years. The demographics of Southville are very similar to those of Cheyney High School. Southville is an affluent area with many residents working for the large "tech" and "medical research" companies found in the area. As such, many of the cars in the student parking lot at Cheyney High School are newer and/or more expensive than the vehicles found in the staff parking lot.

Southville is also home to a prestigious private liberal arts university. The university is two blocks from Cheyney High School. This allows for extra opportunities for the students of Cheyney to have access to programs and facilities at the university.

Guiding Questions

1. How could Ms. Tyson have handled the situation differently?
2. What does Ms. Tyson's "selective hearing" regarding previous incidents tell you about the culture at Cheyney High School?
3. How would this scenario have been handled differently if Stephanie was Black?
4. Would (Should) this scenario have been handled differently if James were Black?
5. Does Stephanie's experience at the principal's office give you any additional insight regarding power and priorities at Cheyney High School?

Please take the time to truly consider the situation and how you might address the circumstances presented. You may use the Case Study Analysis Protocol sheet (Figure 7.1) that follows to help you work through the steps. Once you have completed your analysis of how you (as Mr. Lee, the principal) might proceed (and possible discussion), take a look at the "So, What Happened?" section to see how the scenario actually played out (but don't peek!!!!). The "So What

Happened?" section is not meant to assess or judge any decisions or the individuals involved, it is just a recounting of what actually happened in the scenarios.

READ

Critically read through the entire Case Study and then go back and re-read it. Make notes and/or highlight important facts or issues to be addressed. Define the problems that need to be addressed.

REMOVE

Once the READ phase is complete, REMOVE yourself from the situation. Take a break from the Case Study – and then contemplate...

RESTATE

With a clear mind, go back and RESTATE or summarize the Case Study as if explaining it to a trusted colleague or peer. Focus on and share the pertinent facts. Explain and elaborate on what the "problems" (or "possibilities") are.
Who are the victims? Are there any "unintentional" victims?

REMEDIES

Begin to make a list of possible remedies or courses of action. Do not stop with the first or best "solution". Even if, at first blush the solution appears to be "not a great choice" include it on your list. Truly brainstorm.

How would each be implemented? Who would be involved? Describe the steps that would be taken

RESPOND

Respond to the Case Study by selecting the best possible solution. It is vital to not only explain the solution but to also explain the "why" behind that solution. Elaborate on who the solution helps and how it addresses the various issues (both at the surface and below).

Identify and discuss any possible issues or pitfalls.

Figure 7.1 The 5R Case Study Analysis Protocol

So, What Happened?

Stephanie refused to sit back and just let things be. She sent Mr. Lee a heartfelt and passionately worded email Friday after school explaining what happened earlier in English class and about how "this was wrong" and should not be tolerated.

Friday evening after the football game – which Cheyney High School won – Mr. Lee sat down on his couch to relax after another long day. He glanced at his phone and even though he knew better than to check his email before going to bed (because there was always an "issue" waiting for him to address that he could do nothing about until the next day, at the earliest), he checked his email and saw Stephanie's email. He wouldn't get much sleep tonight.

Mr. Lee was in his second year as principal at Cheyney. He had been a principal at a smaller high school in another district for six years prior to coming to Cheyney. He has noticed multiple issues at Cheyney and has been systematically addressing them. One of the biggest issues he has encountered is the thought that "this is just what we do" and often the feelings of entitlement by students, families, and staff. In his opinion, there is often a lack of urgency regarding helping and supporting students, especially if those students come from underrepresented populations or are not part of the "established" Cheyney hierarchy powerbase. This was another example – another horrible and unacceptable example.

Mr. Lee felt that, like many communities and schools, Cheyney had "talked the good fight" concerning diversity and inclusion. In light of recent high-profile incidents throughout the country, Cheyney had conducted "sensitivity" training for staff and held multicultural assemblies and events. Driving to school each morning it was not uncommon for Mr. Lee to see signs with the phrases "No Hate Here," "Black Lives Matter," and "Cheyney – Home for All" in the yards of the homes surrounding school. But Mr. Lee wasn't convinced that the words and events held were real and part of the core beliefs of the school and community. As he examined data, he still saw the large discrepancies regarding graduation rates, college acceptance rates, discipline rates, and special education classification rates of Black and Latinx students. Just like Stephanie, Mr. Lee was not going to let this go.

First thing Monday morning he had his secretary call Stephanie down to see him. As Stephanie arrived, a red-faced and flushed secretary told Stephanie that Mr. Lee would see her immediately. Mr. Lee apologized to Stephanie that she was not able to see him on Friday when the incident happened. He told her that was not acceptable and that his secretary now knows that if a student needs him for an emergency she needs to get in contact with him immediately (that would explain the secretary's red face). As Stephanie voiced her concerns about the incident, Mr. Lee intently took notes and asked follow-up questions throughout. Once finished, Mr. Lee informed Stephanie that he would immediately investigate the situation. He assured her that even though he may not be allowed to tell her how things would be handled from a disciplinary standpoint (due to confidentiality), he would absolutely address the situation. Stephanie felt reassured and thanked Mr. Lee for taking her concern seriously.

Mr. Lee then met with Ms. Tyson. He asked her to explain what happened on Friday. Ms. Tyson explained the incident along the same lines as what Stephanie had detailed. She concluded that she had "handled things" and that "all was fine now." Mr. Lee sternly informed her that he disagreed. He verbally reprimanded her for not reporting the incident to the office immediately.

A shocked Ms. Tyson countered with "why was this a big deal when none of those kids (Black students) even voiced a problem with it?" This sent Mr. Lee even more over the edge as he said that just because the students don't come to her with a problem doesn't mean that there isn't one. The fact that they don't come to her or other staff probably shows that they don't feel comfortable speaking with her or valued by her and that they don't believe she would do anything to help them. He began to reference Muted Group Theory to her, but she interrupted him.

MS. TYSON: "That's ridiculous! Of course I would help my students no matter what color they are. If I knew of an incident, I would immediately help them and make sure it didn't happen again."

MR. LEE: "Really? Did you do that for *those* students on Friday? You just reinforced the belief to them that no one really cares. Actions speak louder than words!"

Next, Mr. Lee went to speak to the athletic director, Mr. Peace, about the music in the locker room. When Mr. Lee asked Mr. Peace about the music and song in particular,

Mr. Peace said he didn't recall but that the kids play all kinds of "crazy" songs in the locker room. Mr. Lee then spoke to the football coach and told him to make sure the inappropriate music stopped being played in the locker room immediately.

As can be expected in the "whisper down the lane" nature of a school, staff began to hear about Mr. Lee's response regarding the situation. Some felt he was making "too big of a deal over nothing." Most staff members were pleased that he was addressing things in the manner that he was, though. Similar incidents had gone on far too long without being addressed, which caused some staff members to feel defeated in their efforts to bring about change and address equity issues and injustices.

Fortunately for Mr. Lee, the superintendent and a majority of the Board of Education members supported his response 100 percent. They recognized that there are "issues" at Cheyney, and in the district as a whole. Of course, there are those that think that things are "good enough" as they are and that we "shouldn't stir up mess" (two board members in particular). But Mr. Lee, and now others, are focused on truly making "Cheyney – home to all."

Side notes – Mr. Lee now has a new secretary (the former one is no longer employed in the district) and the high school has a new athletic director – Mr. Peace retired early.

8

"Credible Threat" – School Safety Case Study

As Lisa Jackson enters her home after work, she is pleasantly surprised to find that her husband has already taken care of dinner. Sure, he just ordered a pizza for her and their daughter before he left for work, but it's one less thing she has to do. As she sits down to grab a slice she sees her fifteen-year-old daughter sitting on the couch scrolling through her phone as typically is her routine. Mary, a tenth grader at Boyer High School, doesn't even stop looking at her phone to greet her mother. Lisa calls her over to have some dinner.

As they begin to eat, Lisa senses that something is bothering Mary. Lisa opens the door by asking Mary, "How was school today?"

MARY: "Just the same nonsense as always."
          Lisa is a little surprised because Mary is a good
          student (all A's and B's) and doesn't normally
          express any concerns regarding school.
LISA: "What do you mean? What happened?"
MARY: "They are just at it again! It's never gonna change!!"
LISA: "Who? What do you mean?"
MARY: "Those White kids!"

And with that, Mary shows her mother an Instagram video post from one of the White students at Boyer High School. The face of the student is partially blurred out. In the video, the student makes several statements against various groups of students (Black, Latinx, Jewish, and so on) and then says that "all those ni**ers must die." The video appears to be taken in a classroom at the school. Mary tells her mom that it looks like it was even filmed in her history classroom.

Lisa is understandably upset and angry. She tells Mary that they are going to get to the bottom of this and not to worry. She is going to notify the school and the administration immediately.

Mary just looks at her mother and lets out a sarcastic laugh.

MARY: "You don't need to call the school or anything. Everyone knows who it was because the video was posted yesterday during school. Several students told the vice principal, Mr. Burke, yesterday. And the boy was still in school today. That man doesn't care! None of them care!"

Lisa is enraged. She has Mary show her the video again and the numerous posts from various people (both students and adults) commenting on it. She calls several of the other parents she knows and they are all at a lost regarding the posting and the apparent lack of response from the school. She even calls a teacher that she personally knows in the district and the teacher confirms that the student in question was in school today and that nothing has been done from a discipline standpoint as of yet.

Frustrated, angry, and afraid, Lisa next makes two final phone calls for the night. One to the local branch of the NAACP and one to the local police department.

The next morning, Mrs. Hitchner, the principal of Boyer High School, arrives at school and enters her office to begin her normal routine of checking emails and voicemails. She snuck out a little early yesterday for a doctor's appointment so she's already prepared for the extra amount of emails and voicemails that she will need to respond to. She is not prepared to see and hear the messages regarding this situation though. She is shocked and at a loss. Looks like she is going to have to talk with the superintendent, Dr. Momba.

Background Regarding Boyer High School

Boyer High School is the only high school in the Boyer Regional School District. The student population is made up from students in the borough of Boyer, who attend the local elementary and middle school, as well as students from two sending districts, Ashbury and Plainston. Approximately 75 percent of the students come from Boyer, 15 percent from Ashbury, and 10 percent from Plainston. Boyer High School is considered the best high school in this small rural county consisting of five high schools in all. As such, it is a desired destination for many in the county. When compared to other schools outside of the county, though, Boyer typically ranks in the "middle of the pack" with those schools of similar profiles.

There have been several "incidents" in the past relating to race and/or diversity issues. As a result, the Boyer Regional School District has implemented several initiatives surrounding diversity, equity, and inclusion. The elementary and middle school principals have been very involved with these initiatives. There are no such initiatives underway in either Ashbury or Plainston school districts though. To the contrary, when one of the prior racial incidents at the high school involved a student from Ashbury as the perpetrator, the student's father reminded the Boyer superintendent that, "You know, we teach our kids southern values around here."

Student Demographics

Total students (9–12) – 962
85 percent White
9 percent Black
5 percent Latinx
1 percent Asian
39 percent free/reduced lunch
38 percent special education classification
58 percent of graduating seniors attend four-year colleges/ universities

Staff Demographics

10 percent of staff members have four or less years in the district
54 percent of staff members have twenty or more years in the district
98 percent White
1 percent Black
1 percent Asian

The borough of Boyer is a quaint historic community with a population of 9,200 and is surrounded by farmland. There has been a recent influx of new residents due to several new higher-end housing developments. Boyer is approximately twenty minutes from a large metropolitan area, so many of the new homes are being bought by individuals who are completely new to the area and commute to the "city" for work.

The towns of Ashbury and Plainston are smaller in population (1,900 and 1,200, respectively) and considered even more rural and "country."

Guiding Questions

1. What does Mary's comment to her mother – "They are just at it again! It's never gonna change!!" – tell you about how Mary really feels about the school climate at Boyer High School?
2. Does the fact that the video in question is still posted online over a full day after it was reported to administration tell you anything?
3. Based on what you know, do you think the situation would have been handled differently at one of the other Boyer School District schools? Why or why not?
4. How does the fact that Boyer High School includes students from two other sending districts affect this situation?
5. In your opinion, should Mrs. Jackson have called the police? The NAACP? Why or why not?

Please take the time to truly consider the situation and how you might address the circumstances presented. You may use the Case Study Analysis Protocol sheet (Figure 8.1) that follows to help you work through the steps. Once you have completed your analysis of how you (as Dr. Momba, the superintendent) might proceed (and possible discussion), take a look at the "So, What Happened?" section to see how the scenario actually played out (but don't peek!!!!).

The "So What Happened?" section is not meant to assess or judge any decisions or the individuals involved, it is just a recounting of what actually happened in the scenarios.

READ

Critically read through the entire Case Study and then go back and re-read it. Make notes and/or highlight important facts or issues to be addressed. Define the problems that need to be addressed.

REMOVE

Once the READ phase is complete, REMOVE yourself from the situation. Take a break from the Case Study – and then contemplate...

RESTATE

With a clear mind, go back and RESTATE or summarize the Case Study as if explaining it to a trusted colleague or peer. Focus on and share the pertinent facts. Explain and elaborate on what the "problems" (or "possibilities") are.
Who are the victims? Are there any "unintentional" victims?

REMEDIES

Begin to make a list of possible remedies or courses of action. Do not stop with the first or best "solution". Even if, at first blush the solution appears to be "not a great choice" include it on your list. Truly brainstorm.

How would each be implemented? Who would be involved? Describe the steps that would be taken

RESPOND

Respond to the Case Study by selecting the best possible solution. It is vital to not only explain the solution but to also explain the "why" behind that solution. Elaborate on who the solution helps and how it addresses the various issues (both at the surface and below).

Identify and discuss any possible issues or pitfalls.

Figure 8.1 The 5R Case Study Analysis Protocol

94

So, What Happened?

First, yes, this really happened!

After her initial shock, Mrs. Hitchner calls the super-intendent, Dr. Momba, and the vice principal, Mr. Burke. Mrs. Taylor is in her third year as the principal at the high school. Previously, she was the principal at the Boyer Elementary School for four years and is entering her thirty-eighth year in education. Dr. Momba is entering his second year as superintendent and has spearheaded the new diversity-centered initiatives in the district. Mr. Burke is in his sixth year as vice principal. Prior to entering administration, Mr. Burke taught physical education at Boyer High School and is a graduate of Boyer High School.

Dr. Momba calls an immediate meeting with Mrs. Hitchner and Mr. Burke. He is furious that he is just finding out about this incident now – two days after it was reported to Mr. Burke. Mrs. Hitchner explains that she just found out about it as well. This doesn't help quell Dr. Momba's anger as he can't understand how she wouldn't know that something like this has happened in her school.

DR. MOMBA: "How in the hell do you not know that this has occurred? Are you that out of touch with what is occurring in your school?"

He becomes even angrier when he discovers that she left early yesterday without permission or without completing the necessary paperwork for time-off.

Dr. Momba then directs his focus on Mr. Burke. Mr. Burke is rather surprised by all of, in his words, "the fuss." He explains that he addressed the situation. He received the information regarding the post and looked into the situation. Mr. Burke states that since the video was "kinda fuzzy," you really can't tell who it was, so there was really nothing he could do. Besides, the student that the other students think created the video said it wasn't him.

MR. BURKE: "[P]lus, he's a good kid. He's on the wrestling team and his family are good people. Besides, it doesn't even seem like a real threat."

Dr. Momba unleashes his fury on Mr. Burke loud enough so that everyone in the main office (and adjacent hallway) hears the message. He explains that in no way should this have been handled in this manner and that this is completely unacceptable, especially since they have discussed prior incidents similar in nature that have occurred here in the high school. He leaves the meeting to go back to the central office to deal with the police chief and the NAACP president, who are both now waiting for him at his office. He informs Mrs. Hitchner and Mr. Burke to address the situation with the student body and to reach out to students/witnesses for statements so that a thorough investigation can be done.

Fast forward – a little after the last lunch period of the day, Mrs. Taylor addresses the students over the public address speaker. She proceeds to read a fifteen-second statement with a very shaky and nervous tone. She says that "we do not condone hatred here" and that "we all need to embrace each other." She does not mention why she is addressing the students or the incident in particular. Some of the students know what she is talking about, but many have no idea. None of the teachers address her comments with their students and just proceed as normal with their classes. No other comments or communication are made or directed to the students or parents in the days that follow.

Mr. Burke questions several of the students who reported the video post. They all point back to one student as the culprit, Tommy. Tommy denies the accusations again to Mr. Burke. The next day, after an uproar from many of the students in the know, Tommy changes his story and admits that he created and posted the video. He states that he made it in his US History classroom during school before the teacher entered the classroom for that class period, but while several other students were in the classroom with him. Tommy receives one day of out-of-school suspension and two days of internal suspension as his discipline. His parents appeal the consequences. Since the appeal goes to the superintendent, Dr. Momba, their appeal is denied.

The Boyer Police Department met with Dr. Momba for approximately thirty minutes. Dr. Momba shows the video to the police chief. The police chief recognizes the student right away as "Tommy." The chief informs Dr. Momba that they "will look into the situation." After not hearing anything for the rest of the day, Dr. Momba contacts the police chief the next day to inquire about the progress of the investigation. The police chief informs Dr. Momba that the investigation is closed and that the video was "deemed not to be a credible threat." It is after being informed of this information, four days after the incident, that the NAACP president informs the media of the situation. The incident and response (or lack thereof) is a leading story both in print and on TV for the next two days.

Two weeks after the incident, there is a fight involving several students at Charlotte High School when one student (from Ashbury) expresses his frustration with why it's such a "big deal if you call someone a ni**er." There are currently several civil rights complaints against the school district being investigated and two lawsuits involving the district and its actions. At a recent home soccer game at Boyer High School, members of the opposing school reported being called several racial slurs throughout the game. The reported comments came from the student section of the Boyer fans.

Dr. Momba has left the district for another school district with more diversity and in a "less rural" (his words) setting. Mrs. Taylor retired as principal at the end of the school year. Mr. Burke is being considered as her replacement and seems to have the inside track to the principal position.

9

The Leadership Journey

Often the decisions leaders make revert back to their own personal values, beliefs, and ethics. But when considering one's values and ethics, it is vital to distinguish between one's espoused values or ethics of theory and one's ethics of practice (Schein, 2010). Or, to quite simply say it, "actions speak louder than words."

Almost all leaders will tout the fact and "belief" that they care about all students. It's hard to find a school whose mission, vision, or core beliefs statement doesn't include the phrase "all students can learn" or something similar. Unfortunately, these statements are hollow without action. What leaders and districts do means much more than empty catch phrases. It's easy to say these things, but the daily actions of leaders and their practices are what matter. Similar to saying "All Lives Matter" without recognizing that all lives can't matter unless "Black Lives Matter," a leader's espoused values mean nothing without putting them into practice. This takes us to the heart of this equity work. Leaders must take this acquisition of knowledge, concepts, and inequities beyond that of just knowledge. Leaders must put them into practice. It is time for leaders to offer solutions not just announce problems. They must lean into the discomfort and act during this journey toward social justice leadership.

As stated in previous chapters, this process of understanding and implementing equity-based practices and leadership is an ongoing process. As a researched practioner, one must not only accept but also embrace the fact that there is still more to learn and add to one's leadership toolkit. The attempt has been made to give the reader a basic understanding. In this chapter, an introduction to some more in-depth theories and concepts is presented. The hope is that this introduction spurs each researched practioner to engage in further learning and research to gain a deeper understanding of the said concepts. It would be irresponsible and a monumental disservice to pretend that the short introductions that follow are comprehensive of each topic. They are but the tip of the iceberg for each. The hope is that they entice the reader to explore more deeply in their role as a researched practioner.

> *Our ability to reach unity in diversity will be the beauty and the test of our civilization.*　　　　Mahatma Gandhi

Intersectionality

The challenges faced by a Black student in a school district can be overwhelming to say the least. What if that Black student is also female? The challenges encountered as a female student coupled with being Black are obviously greater in scope and number that she must then overcome. She has more things "stacked" against her. She has a heavier load to bear. In addition, what if she is gay ... or a non-native language learning ... or ... classified ... or ....

The intersection of the challenges faced by being a part of different oppressed groups causes a unique set of barriers and as such requires specific supports and structures for those affected. The Oxford Dictionary defines intersectionality as "the network of connections between social categories such as race, class and gender, especially when this may result in additional disadvantage or discrimination." Intersectionality was presented first by professor, legal scholar, and civil rights activist Kimberle Crenshaw in 1989 when examining the struggle of Black women in particular. Crenshaw stressed that traditional feminist ideas and antiracist policies exclude Black women due to the fact that they face overlapping discrimination unique to them. Crenshaw stated that "because the intersectional experience is greater than the sum of racism and sexism, any analysis that does not take intersectionality into account cannot sufficiently address the particular manner in which Black women are subordinated" (Perlman, 2018).

It is easy to see how the concept applies to all who are or have been oppressed. Intersectionality is the acknowledgment that everyone has their own unique experiences of discrimination. We must in turn consider all aspects and experiences of oppression and anything that can marginalize individuals – gender, race, class, sexual orientation, physical ability, and so on. Without an intersectional lens, any attempt to address inequalities and injustice is likely to be in vain and end up perpetuating systems of inequality. Intersectionality is a lens through which one can see where power resides and collides within society, where it interlocks and intersects with the individual experience.

With the increased use of the term, intersectionality is sometimes bastardized and used inappropriately. Like most things, when taken out of context and applied without thought or concern, the concept of intersectionality when used as a blanket term drifts from its true meaning and purpose. Crenshaw warns:

> Some people look to intersectionality as a grand theory of everything, but that's not my intention. If someone is trying to think about how to explain to the courts why they should not dismiss a case made by black women, just because the employer did hire blacks who were men and women who were white, well, that's what the tool was designed to do. If it works, great. If it doesn't work, it's not like you have to use this concept.
>
> The other issue is that intersectionality can get used as a blanket term to mean, "Well, it's complicated." Sometimes, "It's complicated" is an excuse not to do anything. At AAPF and the Center for Intersectionality and Social Policy Studies, we want to move beyond that idea. (2017)

Social Justice Leadership

The educational leaders of today are faced with unprecedented challenges. Social justice issues, COVID-19, and the overall confrontational nature of society make leading schools and learning an oftentimes overwhelming calling. The focus of leaders in P–12 schools must be on creating safe, equitable learning environments for all students – regardless of their race, disability, sexual orientation, or developmental challenges. The times are challenging and our leaders must be up for the challenges that await.

Of course, the concept of social justice is not a new one. Various scholars have offered their versions of definitions for social justice as it relates to schools. For example:

- Make issues of race, class, gender, disability, sexual orientation, and other historically and currently marginalized conditions in the US central to the advocacy, leadership practice, and vision (Theoharis, 2007).
- "[T]he concept of social justice focuses on ... [t]hose groups that are most often underserved, underrepresented, and undereducated and that face various forms of oppression in schools" (Dantley and Tillman, 2010).
- Social justice requires a more complete understanding of the social (in)justice issues in schools, the community, and the world in which students live now and in which they will work as thoughtful, contributing adults (Shields, 2010).

Paolo Freire's seminal work *Pedagogy of the Oppressed* (1970) gives the first, and perhaps most complete, exploration of how the practice of social justice leadership can address the systemic barriers that face entire groups of students. Developing a true understanding of others and their traveled paths can lead to an enlightened leadership that can reach untapped levels of growth and potential success for all.

Freire offers his tenets of social justice education as a guide (1970). The first stresses the importance of developing awareness of oppressive social conditions. Look and listen to others, their surroundings, and the role played by others. Second, individuals must develop a self-awareness which includes how one's power and privilege affect one's own world view. Not everyone has the same experiences or obstacles. How does one's privilege, or lack thereof, change one's daily interactions, expectations, and even dreams? The final tenet is realizing and accepting that there is a need for social action. This must be embraced by all, not just by a select few. As the great author Maya Angelou so aptly stated, "It is time for parents to teach young people early on that in diversity, there is beauty, and there is strength."

For school leaders, leadership for social justice is conceived as praxis, in the Freireian sense, involving both reflection and action. It spans multiple dimensions, which serve as arenas for this praxis. These dimensions include the personal, interpersonal, communal, systemic, and ecological. Each dimension within the framework requires the development of capacities on the part of the leader, capacities for both reflection and action (Furman, 2012).

Furman goes on to categorize the nature of social justice leadership using the following key characteristics:

- **Action Oriented** – Social justice leaders are proactive change agents engaged in "transformative leadership."
- **Committed and Persistent** – Deeply committed to a social justice agenda and are often stubborn in their persistence.
- **Inclusive and Democratic** – Practice deep collaboration with parents, community, and integrated learning environments for all students, including special education students.
- **Relational and Caring** – Social justice leaders work to develop and maintain caring relationships based in authentic communication.

- **Reflective** – Engage in critical self-reflective practice aimed at personal awareness and growth (they not only reflect but also take action as a result of their reflection).
- **Oriented toward a Socially Just Pedagogy** – The continuous examination that instruction and student learning are equitable for all student groups (2012).

As referenced by Furman, the social justice leader practices transformative leadership as well. This is important because leadership "must be critically educative; it can not only look at the conditions in which we live, but it must also decide how to change them" (Foster, 1986). Leadership is not stagnant. It must remain fluid and responsive. More specifically, as Weiner (2003) expresses, "transformative leadership is an exercise of power and authority that begins with questions of justice, democracy, and the debate between individual accountability and social responsibility."

Transformative leadership is not the same as transformational leadership. While transformational leadership can be effective in motivating others toward a specific school or district goal, transformative leadership goes further. Its scope and sphere of influence goes beyond the school house walls and affects the community and society as a whole (Figure 9.1).

Adverse Childhood Experiences

It is not uncommon to hear leaders and educators tout the fact that they are getting their students ready for "the real world." They are usually describing how their strict rules, procedures,

Transformational or Transformative?

Transformational Leadership	Transformative Leadership
• Raises the level of motivation and morality of followers	• Challenges inappropriate uses of power and privilege
• Helps leaders and followers reach their fullest potential	• Addresses the need for social betterment
• Strives to reach organizational goals and objectives	• Begins with questions of justice and democracy

* Transformative leadership extends beyond the school house walls.

Figure 9.1 Transformational or transformative leadership

and/or timelines are preparing students for "life" and for when things aren't "easy" like they are now for their students.

Describing the lives of students as "easy" couldn't be further from the truth. The fact is that many students are experiencing things and living in circumstances that many of their teachers and administrators would never be able to survive. Unfortunately, many young people know the "real world" far more intimately than they should ever have to.

The experiences, exposure, and opportunities (or lack thereof) of an individual greatly influence their future. Student trauma and its effects can be studied by examining Adverse Childhood Experiences (ACEs). The term ACE originated in a groundbreaking study conducted in 1995 by the Centers for Disease Control and the Kaiser Permanente health care organization in California. Research has shown that ACEs can have a "tremendous" impact on a young person's future (CDC, 2020).

ACEs are potentially traumatic events that occur during childhood (zero to seventeen years), in addition to environmental conditions that undermine a child's sense of safety, stability, and fairness. The greater number of ACEs a child experiences, the more "at-risk" he/she is – ACEs can have lasting, negative effects on health, well-being, and opportunity (CDC, 2020). As research has grown from the original study, scholars agree that exposure to racism, discrimination, stigma, minority stress, and historical trauma should be considered when discussing ACEs (Lanier, 2020). Early experiences of racism have measurable and broad negative impacts on health (Williams and Williams-Morris, 2000; Chae, Drenkard, Lewis, and Lim, 2015).

Discrimination, isolation, and racism definitely affect ACE scores for young people. Children who have experienced interpersonal discrimination are at higher risk of exposure to institutional/systemic racism and these children have higher rates of ACEs (Lanier, 2020). Racism and the perception of racism have lasting effects (Williams and Williams-Morris, 2000). These effects last well past school age and manifest themselves in adulthood where they can range from heart disease and birth defects to higher levels of incarceration and mental illness (Kim, Kuendig, Prasad, and Sexter, 2020).

Leaders should be working together to create communities and schools where "every child can thrive" (CDC, 2020). This cannot be achieved through neglect, abandonment, or state-sponsored invisibleness of any student or group of students. Doing so would result in intensified feelings of isolation and inferiority. This would increase already-existing feelings of distrust and betrayal of the institutional and systematic structures of society. The negative racial, gender, classification, and class impacts would be significant and the associated symbolic losses would be, quite frankly, impossible to overcome.

Muted Group Theory

> We don't have a (fill in the blank – race, gender, LGBTQ+, drug . . .) issue here. I've never had a student even bring up a concern or problem. We all just get along so well.

A version of that statement or something similar is quite common in schools and made by administrators and teachers whenever "controversial" issues are mentioned. And while it may be true that there are few, if any, complaints or concerns brought to leaders concerning these topics, it is often a reflection of a culture where some groups feel as if voicing their concerns would be fruitless. The perception, and oftentimes based on reality and past experiences, is that their concerns will be brushed aside and not taken seriously. Members of oppressed groups have "learned" that it is best to just keep quiet because no one (in charge) really cares.

Muted group theory is a concept first articulated by anthropologists Ardener and Ardener in the 1960s and 1970s. The theory was originally used to explain gender differences, but it has subsequently been applied to other identity groups, including racial identity. At its core, muted group theory is the basic idea that throughout society there are cultural groups that are traditionally muted – ones that are given less access than members of the dominant groups to public discourse and to having their concerns heard or valued (Meares, 2017). Through this concept, there is a hierarchy of dominance, the revelation of acceptability, and ultimately subordination.

Understanding the foundational precepts of muted group theory can facilitate the change and inclusivity so desperately needed throughout schools and districts. Leaders must grasp that identity and reality are socially constructed. They must then comprehend the fact that communication is the means for that construction. Once done, organizations will have no choice but to acknowledge that members of muted groups have had to adjust to the dominant ways of communication to get their voices heard. Only then can the realization and promise that resistance and change are possible be attained.

Critical Theories

As recently as just a few years ago, the overwhelming dialogue regarding what schools, and in turn students, need to "be better at" surrounded around the concept of "critical thinking." The concept, first taught by Socrates, involves an objective analysis and evaluation of a problem or situation in order to offer a course of action or to form a judgment. Both the public and private sectors voiced concern that the future workforce needed to be better critical thinkers. They need to do more than just follow a checklist. They need to be able to analyze and examine a concept or situation in a rational and unbiased manner. Being critical thinkers was a must.

Fast forward to today and it seems quite ironic that just by adding the word "race" (Critical Race Theory (CRT)) to the words "critical" and "theory" one can cause such a firestorm and uproar in certain circles. Something that was such a nonnegotiable (critical thinking) and a must-have could now be considered abhorrent and even "un-American" by some when it was used to examine race.

Critical Theory itself has its roots in sociology and is any approach that focuses on reflective assessment and the critique of society and culture to reveal inequities and challenges power structures. Formally defined by the likes of Fromm and Horkheimer in the 1930s, Critical Theory is a construct oriented toward critiquing and changing societal standing and hierarchy. Horkheimer described it as a theory that seeks "to liberate human beings from the circumstances that enslave them" (Horkheimer, 1982, 244).

There are various "critical theories" that have evolved from this basic pretense. A brief overview of some of the most prominent are presented here, each of which follows the same basic principles. They seek to relieve suffering and oppression. Each relies on the moral and ethical leadership of those in charge to strive for social justice. They begin with a critique of educational policy and practice to assess how oppression is addressed or perpetuated. There is a determined focus on sharing power to disrupt oppression and inequity. And lastly, political leadership is required to lead and encourage a dialogue regarding problems of practice and the true change needed to correct them.

Critical Race Theory

First the facts. Critical Race Theory originated in the field of legal studies as a means to address the racial realities of people of color in the United States. The goal of CRT was to provide a "voice" to racially marginalized populations from a legal studies perspective (Ladson-Billings and Tate, 1995).

The theory proposes that racism is "normal and pervasive" and therefore has been internalized in American culture. As a result, race has become a social construct that determines equity, or the lack thereof. Critical Race Theory provides a theoretical approach to understanding systematic racism in the United States. Through this understanding, CRT suggests that growth and true equity could be attained, but only after much work and self-reckoning.

The depth and complexities of the topic and theory make CRT a topic that is above the level of school-aged children. It is not something that is or could be taught in P–12 schools. Again, it originated as part of legal studies (Law School) and is not typically studied or taught in earnest until such terminal degree levels.

Critical Race Theory paved the way for other theories such as LatCrit, Tribal Crit, Black Crit, and Asian Crit.

Critical Disability Theory

Critical Disability Theory (CDT) is a framework for the analysis of what "disability" is and challenges the assumptions which shape society. Critical Disability Theory encompasses a diverse set of theoretical approaches. The theory is anchored in Disability Rights activism, which led to the Americans with Disabilities Act of 1992.

At its core, the purpose of CDT is to analyze disability as a cultural, historical, relative, social, and political phenomenon. Critical Disability Theory can also be referenced as "critical disability studies" (CDS) (e.g., Meekosha and Shuttleworth, 2009; Vehmas and Watson, 2014). Critical Disability Theory is a methodology, not a "subject-oriented area of study" (Schalk, 2017). As a methodology, the theory involves examining the social norms that define particular attributes as impairments, as well as the social conditions that concentrate stigmatized attributes in particular populations.

Critical Disability Theory advocates for both accommodation and equality for disabled individuals. It is important to view disability as a lived reality in which the experience of individuals with disabilities becomes central to interpreting their own reality. Critical Disability Theory challenges traditional notions of special education and medical models that view disabilities from a deficit perspective.

Critical Feminist Theory

The term critical modifies feminist theory, suggesting that all feminist theory criticizes the misogynistic view of women found throughout society. Thus, feminist theory, viewed in this light, is a critical theory representing the radical notion that women are people (Clark, 2007).

Critical Feminist Theory investigates the influence of social constructs and norms of gender and gender-specific interest and experiences. It forces an examination of how ALL students can be served in today's education system.

Critical Feminist Theory is particularly focused on the perspective of marginalized populations in education and attempts to address gender and intersections of gender (intersectionality), including race, ethnicity, socioeconomic status, sexual orientation, and ability status (Pratt-Clark, 2010). The theory encompasses many "modified" feminist theories, indicating a multiplicity of theories critical of feminism itself. These theories can push the original concept of feminism to recognize a deeper sense of radicalism.

(Critical) Queer Theory

Queer Theory critically examines the way power works to institutionalize and legitimate certain forms and expressions of sexuality and gender (Ruhsam, 2017). This examination of and reflection on societal norms reveals that homophobia and heterosexism are pervasive and "normal" thoughts. Queer theory attempts to disrupt these "normal" perceptions and accepted beliefs (Ruhsam, 2017).

The theory reveals the pervasiveness of heteronormativity and suggests that anti-queer bias is deeply engrained in educational law and policy. Methods to combat these biases involve resistance with the goal of liberating oppressed populations. There must be consideration as to how language is used to marginalize people (Capper, 2019). As with all critical theories, with Queer theory there needs to be an understanding of intersectionality and how the theory draws from and/or links to tenets of other critical theories (Capper, 2019).

As previously stated, this is just the beginning. To think that "you have this equity stuff mastered" through the reading of one section, or one chapter, or one text would be irresponsible and delusional. The work is hard and complex. The topic is absolutely a heavy lift. But it is a topic that must be addressed and one that must be addressed repeatedly with fidelity. The researched practioner must dedicate the time and effort to learn and to constantly grow in this work because it is worth it. Because today's students deserve it and because they are worth it. Press on!

"No Progress without Struggle"

by Frederick Douglass

(*An excerpt from his August 1857 address concerning "West India Emancipation"*)

Let me give you a word of the philosophy of reforms. The whole history of the progress of human liberty shows that all concessions, yet made to her august claims, have been born of earnest struggle . . .

If there is no struggle, there is no progress. Those who profess to favor freedom and yet depreciate agitation are men who want crops without plowing the ground. They want rain without thunder and lightning. They want the ocean without the roar of its mighty waters.

The struggle may be a moral one or it may be a physical one, or it may be both moral and physical, but it must be a struggle. Power concedes nothing without a demand. It never has and it never will. Find out just what a people will submit to, and you have found out the exact amount of injustice and wrong which will be imposed upon them; and these will continue till they are resisted with either words or blows, or with both. The limits of tyrants are pre-scribed by the endurance of those whom they oppress.

Men may not get all they pay for in this world, but they must pay for all they get. If we ever get free from the oppression and wrongs heaped upon us, we must pay for their

removal. We must do this by labor, by suffering, by sacrifice, and, if needs be, by our lives and the lives of others.
(Frederick Douglass, "No Progress without Struggle," available from *The W. E. B. DuBois Learning Center*, www.duboislc.org/html/BlackStruggle.html.)

Aikin, W. M. (1942). *The Story of the Eight-Year Study: With Conclusions and Recommendations.* New York: Harper & Bros.

American Association of School Administrators (AASA). (February 10, 2020). AASA Releases Key Findings from American Superintendent 2020 Decennial Study. www.aasa.org/content.aspx?id=44397.

Ansell, S. E. (December 14, 2011). *Achievement Gap.* Education Week. Retrieved April 11, 2022, from www.edweek.org/leadership/achievement-gap/2004/09.

Berliner, D. C. (2006). Our Impoverished View of Educational Research. *Teachers College Record,* 108(6), 949–995. https://doi.org/10.1111/j.1467-9620.2006.00682.x.

Berliner, D. C. (2009). *Poverty and Potential: Out-of-School Factors and School Success.* Boulder and Tempe: Education and the Public Interest Centre & Education Policy Research Unit.

Capper, C. A. (2019). *Organizational Theory for Equity and Diversity: Leading Integrated Socially Just Education.* Routledge.

CDC (Center for Disease Control and Prevention) (2020). Adverse Childhood Experiences(ACEs). https://cdc.gov/violenceprevention/aces/index.html.

Chae, D. H., Drenkard, C. M., Lewis, T. T., & Lim, S. S. (2015). Discrimination and Cumulative Disease Damage among African American Women with Systemic Lupus Erythematosus. *American*

Journal of Public Health, 105(10), 2099–2107. https://doi.org/10.2105/
AJPH.2015.302727.

Chin, J. (2010). Introduction to the Special Issue on Diversity and
Leadership. *The American Psychologist*, 65, 150–156. https://doi
.org/10.1037/a0018716.

Clark, D. S. (2007). Critical Feminist Theory. In *Encyclopedia of Law
& Society: American and Global Perspectives*, Vol. 1, pp. 349–350.
Newbury Park, CA: Sage. https://doi.org/10.4135/9781412952637
.n150.

Crenshaw, K. (2017). Kimberlé Crenshaw on Intersectionality, More
than Two Decades Later. *Columbia Law School.* www.law.columbia
.edu/news/archive/kimberle-crenshaw-intersectionality-more-two-
decades-later.

Dantley, M. E., & Tillman, L. C. (2010). Social Justice and Moral
Transformative Leadership. In C. Marshall & O. Maricela (Eds.)
Leadership for Social Justice, pp. 19–31. Boston, MA: Allyn &
Bacon.

Darling-Hammond, L. (2015). *The Flat World and Education: How
America's Commitment to Equity Will Determine Our Future.*
New York: Teachers College Press.

Davis, L. P., & Museus, S. D. (2019). Identifying and Disrupting
Deficit Thinking. *Medium.* https://medium.com/national-center-
for-institutional-diversity/identifying-and-disrupting-deficit-
thinking-cbc6da326995.

Dewey, J. (1921). *Reconstruction in Philosophy.* London: University
of London Press.

Dickens, W. (2005). Genetic Differences and School Readiness. *The
Future of Children / Center for the Future of Children, the David
and Lucile Packard Foundation*, 15, 55–69.

Douglass, F. (1857). Frederick Douglass Declares There Is "No Progress
without Struggle." *SHEC: Resources for Teachers.* https://shec
.ashp.cuny.edu/items/show/1245.

Du Bois, W. E. B. (1903). *The Souls of Black Folk*. New York: Penguin.

Dugan, J. P. (2017). *Leadership Theory: Cultivating Critical Perspectives*. Hoboken, NJ: Jossey-Bass.

Ed Week (September 25, 2020). Anti-Racist Teaching: What Educators Really Think. Education Week. Retrieved February 1, 2022, from www.edweek.org/leadership/anti-racist-teaching-what-educators-really-think/2020/09.

Felton, E. (September 6, 2017). The Department of Justice Is Overseeing the Resegregation of American Schools. *The Nation*. www.thenation.com/article/archive/the-department-of-justice-is-overseeing-the-resegregation-of-american-schools/.

Ferguson, H., Bovaird, S., & Mueller, M. (2007). The Impact of Poverty on Educational Outcomes for Children. *Paediatrics & Child Health*, 12(8), 701–706. https://doi.org/10.1093/pch/12.8.701.

Fleming, S. M. (September, 2014). The Power of Reflection. *Scientific American Mind*, 25(5), 31–37.

Frederick, D. (1857). No Progress without Struggle. *The W.E.B. DuBois Learning Center*. www.duboislc.org/html/BlackStruggle.html.

Freire, P. (1970). *Pedagogy of the Oppressed*. New York: Seabury Press.

Foster, W. P. (1986). *Paradigms and Promises: New Approaches to Educational Administration*. Amherst, NY: Prometheus Books.

Furman, G. (2012). Social Justice Leadership as Praxis: Developing Capacities through Preparation Programs. *Educational Administration Quarterly*, 48(2), 191–229.

Gibbs, G. (1988). *Learning by Doing: A Guide to Teaching and Learning Methods*. Great Britain: Further Education Unit.

Gorski, P. C., & Pothini, S. G. (2018). *Case Studies on Diversity and Social Justice Education*, 2nd ed. New York:Routledge. https://doi.org/10.4324/9781351142526.

Government Printing Office. (1918). Cardinal Principles of Secondary Education: A Report of the Commission on the Reorganization of Secondary Education, Appointed by the National Education Association. (n.d.).

Graham, S. (2018). Race/Ethnicity and Social Adjustment of Adolescents: How (Not if) School Diversity Matters. *Educational Psychologist*, 53(2), 64–77. https://doi.org/10.1080/00461520.2018.1428805.

Hanushek, E. (2013). *For Each and Every Child: A Strategy for Education Equity and Excellence*. Washington, DC: U.S. Department of Education.

Henson, K. T., & Eller, B. F. (1999). *Educational Psychology for Effective Teaching*. 2nd ed. Belmont, CA: Wadsworth.

Horkheimer, M. (1982). *Critical Theory Selected Essays*. New York: Continuum.

Hussain-Khaliq, S. (n.d.). Learning Case Studies: Definitions and Applications. *The Partnering Initiative*. https://thepartneringinitiative.org/.

Juvonen, J., Kogachi, K. and Graham, S. (2018). When and How Do Students Benefit From Ethnic Diversity in Middle School? *Child Development*, 89, 1268–1282. https://doi.org/10.1111/cdev.12834.

Kim, H., Kuendig, J., Prasad, K. & Sexter, A. (2020). Exposure to Racism and Other Adverse Childhood Experiences Among Perinatal Women with Moderate to Severe Mental Illness. *Community Mental Health Journal*, 56, 1–8. https://doi.org/10.1007/s10597-020-00550-6.

Kite, M. E., & Clark, P. (September 8, 2022). The Benefits of Diversity Education. www.apa.org/ed/precollege/psychology-teacher-network/introductory-psychology/benefits-of-diversity.

Ladson-Billings, G., & Tate, W. F., IV. (1995). Toward a Critical Race Theory of Education. *Teachers College Record*, 97(1), 47–68.

Lanier, P. (July 2, 2020). Racism Is an Adverse Childhood Experience (ACE). *The Jordan Institute for Families.* https://jordaninstituteforfamilies.org/2020/racism-is-an-adverse-childhood-experience-ace/.

Lareau, A. (1987). Social Class Differences in Family-School Relationships: The Importance of Cultural Capital. *Sociology of Education*, 60(2), 73–85. https://doi.org/10.2307/2112583.

Letourneau, N., Anis, L., Ntanda, H., et al. (2020). Attachment & Child Health (ATTACH) Pilot Trials: Effect of Parental Reflective Function Intervention for Families Affected by Toxic Stress. *Infant Mental Health Journal*, 41, 445–462. https://doi.org/10.1002/imhj.21833.

McKillip, M., & Luhm, T. (2020). (rep.). *Investing Additional Resources in Schools Serving Low-Income Students.* Education Law Center. Retrieved March 2, 2022, from https://edlawcenter.org/assets/files/pdfs/publications/Investing_in_Students_Policy_Bri.pdf.

Meares, M. (2017). Muted Group Theory. In Y. Y. Kim (Ed.) *The International Encyclopedia of Intercultural Communication.* Hoboken: John Wiley and Sons. https://doi.org/10.1002/9781118783665.ieicc0228.

Meekosha, H., & Shuttleworth, R. (2009). What's So "Critical" about Critical Disability Studies? *Australian Journal of Human Rights*, 15(1), 47–75. https://doi.org/10.1080/1323238X.2009.11910861.

Merriam-Webster. (n.d.). Introvert. www.merriam-webster.com/dictionary/introvert.

Miller, H. M. (2001). Teaching and Learning about Cultural Diversity: Becoming a Multicultural Teacher. *The Reading Teacher*, 55(4), 346–347. www.jstor.org/stable/20205060.

Oxford University Press. (n.d.). *Oxford Advanced Learner's Dictionary.* www.oxfordlearnersdictionaries.com/.

Payne, K., Niemi, L., & Doris, J. L. (2018). How to Think about "Implicit Bias." *Scientific American.* www.scientificamerican.com/article/how-to-think-about-implicit-bias/.

Perlman, M. (October 23, 2018). The Origin of the Term "Intersectionality." *Columbia Journalism Review.* www.cjr.org/language_corner/intersectionality.php.

Pew Research Center. (2019). Race in America 2019. www.pewresearch.org/social-trends/2019/04/09/race-in-america-2019/.

Pratt-Clarke, M. A. E. (2010). *Critical Race, Feminism, and Education: A Social Justice Model.* New York: Palgrave Macmillan.

Pritlove, C., Juando-Prats, C., Ala-Leppilampi, K., & Parsons, J. A. (2019). The Good, the Bad, and the Ugly of Implicit Bias. *The Lancet,* 393(10171), 502–504.

Ruhsam, J. J. (2017). *Introduction to Queer Theory.* University of Massachusetts.

Schalk, S. (2017). Critical Disability Studies as Methodology. *Lateral,* 6(1).

Schein, E. (2010). *Organizational Culture and Leadership,* 4th ed. The Jossey-Bass Business & Management Series. Hoboken, NJ: Jossey-Bass.

The Schott Foundation. (2016). http://schottfoundation.org/resources.

Senge, P. M. (2000). Strategies for Change Leaders; Lessons for Change Leaders. *Leader to Leader, Drucker Foundation.* Jossey-Bass.

Sergiovanni, T. J. (1987). *The Principalship: A Reflective Practice Perspective.* Newton, MA: Pearson.

Shemla, M. (2022, October 12). Why Workplace Diversity Is So Important, and Why It's So Hard to Achieve. *Forbes.* www.forbes.com/sites/rsmdiscovery/2018/08/22/why-workplace-diversity-is-so-important-and-why-its-so-hard-to-achieve/.

Shields, C. M. (2010). Transformative Leadership: Working for Equity in Diverse Contexts. *Educational Administration Quarterly,* 46(4), 558–589.

Sinek, S. (2011). *Start with Why: How Great Leaders Inspire Everyone to Take Action*. New York: Portfolio.

Slack, K. (2003). Whose Aspirations Are They Anyway? *International Journal of Inclusive Education*, 7(4), 325–335, https://doi.org/10.1080/1360311032000110016.

Smith, J. (August 15, 2017). How Students Benefit from School Diversity. https://greatergood.berkeley.edu/article/item/how_students_benefit_from_school_diversity.

Sparks, S. (June 23, 2011). Study Finds Gaps Remain Large for Hispanic Students. *Education Week*. www.edweek.org/ew/articles/2011/06/23/36hispanic.h30.html.

Stancil, W. (March 14, 2018). School Segregation Is Not a Myth. *The Atlantic*. www.theatlantic.com/education/archive/2018/03/school-segregation-is-not-a-myth/555614/.

Steele, C. M. (1998). Stereotyping and Its Threat Are Real. *American Psychologist*, 53(6), 680–681. https://doi.org/10.1037/0003-066X.53.6.680.

Tanner, D., & Tanner, L. (2007). *Curriculum Development: Theory into Practice*. Upper Saddle River, NJ: Pearson Merrill/Prentice Hall.

Theoharis, G. (2007). Social Justice Educational Leaders and Resistance: Toward a Theory of Social Justice Leadership. *Educational Administration Quarterly*, 43, 221–258.

Tienken, C. & Domenech, D. A. (2020). *The American Superintendent: 2020 Decennial Study*. Seton Hall University Faculty Publications.

Vehmas, S. & Watson, N. (2014). Moral Wrongs, Disadvantages, and Disability: A Critique of Critical Disability Studies. *Disability & Society*, 29. https://doi.org/10.1080/09687599.2013.831751.

Viadero, D. & Johnston, R. (2000). Lifting Minority Achievement: Complex Answers: The Achievement Gap. *Education Week*.

Weiner, E. J. (2003). Secretary Paulo Freire and the Democratization of Power: Toward a Theory of Transformative Leadership. *Educational Philosophy and Theory*, 35(1), 89–106.

Wells, A. S., Fox, L., & Cordova, D. (2016). How Racially Diverse Schools and Classrooms Can Benefit All Students. https://tcf.org/content/report/how-racially-diverse-schools-and-classrooms-can-benefit-all-students/?agreed=1. Accessed September 14, 2018.

Williams, D. & Williams-Morris, R. (2000). Racism and Mental Health: The African American Experience. *Ethnicity & Health*, 5, 243–268. https://doi.org/10.1080/713667453.

Wong, H. K., Wong, R. T., Jondahl, S. F., & Ferguson, O. F. (2014). *The Classroom Management Book*. Mountain View, CA: Harry K. Wong.

Zhao, Y. (2009). *Catching Up or Leading the Way: American Education in the Age of Globalization*. Alexandria, VA: ASCD.

Achievement Gap
  generally, 20–21
  Coleman Report, 21–22
  components of, 23
  deficit thinking, problem of, 21
  defined, 20–21
  levels of, 22
  race and, 22–23
  socio-economic causes of, 23
  statistics, 22
Activists, 41–42, 43
Adverse Childhood Experiences
  (ACEs)
  generally, 105–106
  effects of, 107
  leadership and, 107–108
  origins of, 106
  race and, 107
Advocates, 40–41, 42
African Americans
  case studies relating to (*See* Music
    with racially inappropriate
    lyrics (case study); Threats of
    racial violence(case study))
  Critical Race Theory (CRT)
    and, 111
Allies, 39–40, 42, 43–44
American School Superintendent
  Association, 37

Angelou, Maya, 34, 104
Anthony, Susan B., 41
Ardener, Edwin, 108
Ardener, Shirley, 108
Asians, case studies relating to. *See*
  Teacher hiring (case study)
Autonomy of students, 6–7

Benefits of diversity, 20, 35–37
Black Lives Matter, 99
Bullying, 42

Cardinal Principles of Secondary
  Education, 7
Case studies. *See also specific case
  study*
  analysis of, 10–11 (*See also* Case
    Study Analysis Protocol)
  guiding questions, 10
  Professional Development
    and, 11
  Professional Learning
    Communities (PLC) and, 11
  results ("so, what happened?"), 10
  structure of, 10
  use of, 10–11
Case Study Analysis Protocol
  generally, 12–13, 16–17
  listen phase, 13–14